THROUGH THE
EYES
OF A
SHEEP

Pamela Rene Anders Cook

ISBN 979-8-88644-013-3 (Paperback)
ISBN 979-8-88644-014-0 (Digital)

Copyright © 2024 Pamela Rene Anders Cook
All rights reserved
First Edition

To protect the privacy and respect of the people who were close to me and involved in my life during certain incidents, the names and places have been changed.

All rights reserved. No part of this publication may be reproduced, distributed, or transmitted in any form or by any means, including photocopying, recording, or other electronic or mechanical methods without the prior written permission of the publisher. For permission requests, solicit the publisher via the address below.

Covenant Books
11661 Hwy 707
Murrells Inlet, SC 29576
www.covenantbooks.com

CONTENTS

Preface v
A Child's View 1
School Days: A Teen's View..8
The Invitation: A Sinner's View..28
Invitation Accepted: A New Beginning 34
The Journey Continues: A Sheep's View...............................39
Moving On 47
A Journey Back: Finding My Way Home 54
Becoming One 60
Shaking but Unmovable: Time to Move Forward in God............66
Standing for God: Stay in the Race 71
Finally, Clarity 79
The Conclusion of the Whole Matter: The Beginning of the End.....81
Through the Eyes of a Sheep 84

PREFACE

When I began to write this book over fifteen years ago, my plan was to share with those who would be reading this the dark side of my view about my life as a sinner and my life as a born-again Christian. The wonderful thing about where I am now near the end of 2024 is that my heavenly Father has blessed me to walk closer with him, my King Jesus Christ, and his precious Holy Spirit. The Holy Spirit is leading me in every step with my eyes wide open.

I see now that the words of this book are not to hurt anyone or give high recognition to the darkness of the enemy that we all face sometimes in our lives, our homes, our communities, and the church. I pray that when you read these words, you will be able to feel the experiences that I feel every day as I walk closer with my God, my Savior, and the Holy Spirit.

I truly thank my Heavenly Father, for sending his beloved Son, Jesus Christ, to die for my sins. Through his Holy Spirit, I have come to understand why Apostle Paul said, "Jesus is the author and finisher of his faith." Faith is the most powerful access a person can have because it will determine each step a person will take as a believer in Jesus Christ.

My faith as a believer has helped me to obtain and understand my past, present, and future steps on this Christian journey—a path that will lead to a better and deeper relationship with my Heavenly Father, my Lord Jesus Christ, and the Holy Spirit. I have come to understand when he placed me in my mother's womb, the life I lived before I knew Jesus Christ, God had already planned before I even knew my parents.

There are three major parts that relate to my walk in knowing God the Father. First, I didn't know who God the Father was and his purpose for mankind. Secondly, I learned that God gave his only begotten Son because he so loves the world. Finally, I heard that God wanted to have relationships with his sons and daughters whom he had created in this present world. These were the key points that changed my life, and this was the day my eyes as a sheep of God began to open.

When I began to write this book, I was in a place where I felt that I needed to release the hurt and pain that I had endured over time. However, I realized that God was not ready for me to move forward in sharing my story. So the writing process became dominant. There was still more he had to do for me in illuminating me with understanding and knowledge from above to understand the reason for being here and continuing the journey for his purpose.

The world we live in will cause many effects on how one views the things around them. This can lead to misconceptions and reasonings. Misconceptions can alter the decisions and choices we make and how we live in unity and love one another, especially in the body of Christ.

These experiences have crossed my path in ways that I have responded to the things around me because of the things that I was exposed to. These effects would cause my view to become dimmer, and I began to see things with my emotions.

However, without being aware and having an understanding of the fullness of what was going on around me, I jump-started with my viewing process of my parents, teachers, friends, spiritual leaders, and those who were in authority positions. These views of others played a major role in painting a picture of hope and illusion of how my life was or would end up. This was because these were just elements of my life but not my life. These things only became a crutch, which gave me access in making decisions, whether they were right or wrong, or building things up and breaking things down.

I believe our choices are made on what we see sometimes. This can lead us to undesirable situations and places—places that can make us feel justified or condemned, especially when those choices are based on hurt, pain, and disappointment. This can cause our views and eyes to become dull in seeing the truth and beauty of what God wants us to see in each other.

Yes, we can receive words and ideals from the unique tools that have been designed by God to help us view the things around us, the way he desires us to see, according to his true purpose for mankind. Therefore, I believe understanding the things around us with our eyes wide open is a technique only God can use to help us see as he sees.

Expectations can be extremely complicated, especially when things do not always go the way we hope they go. Daily challenges will confront us throughout our lives. I've learned it is not just how we accept our challenges that matter, but how we face them that could determine our walk with God. I pray when you read the words on these pages, it will encourage and strengthen you in knowing that God delights in opening our eyes to see as he does. This will bring us peace in a time of chaos and light in a time of darkness.

A CHILD'S VIEW

The view of the world was beautiful, and things that my eyes focused on brought pleasure to my imagination. This is when I began to see the things around me, not knowing that there was someone *greater* than me who was placing this in my mind. The green grass, the bright sun, and the stars that shone brightly at night beside the moon gave the brightest light. The flowers and trees that displayed varieties of colors each season left a peaceful picture in my mind.

The colors and smells made me look forward to seeing it again and again every year. Everything around me was beautiful and peaceful. My eyes were pleased, and my heart was content. I was seeing things that God had created yet not understanding the Creator. I did not understand the full meaning of his creation. My understanding was as a child. I thought like a child, and I was doing the things that only a child knew how to do.

The views of my surroundings were pure and innocent. It was with love as I knew it that embedded my mind and heart with a sense of security—views that only a child in his or her pureness could have experienced that seemed to last for a lifetime. I did not know that there would come a point in time when the residue of darkness would shadow the uniqueness of that beauty, and become things that I would carry in my mind trying to capture the fullness that would make me feel whole and secure as I grew older.

How long would the beauty of God's creation last in the mind of a child? Only God could answer that question. My eyes and my heart viewed one way, and my ears heard something different. My soul was sheltered in a body prepared for a journey of expectations in a world that would lead me to the unknown or uncertainties of views that a child could not begin to comprehend. As I grew older, each beautiful day, the Lord blessed me to see my views that gradually began to slowly fade away to reality. It was a belief that a life worth living is a story worth telling.

When I was a little girl, the things around me had definitions and meanings that were structured by my parents. To me, this was my simple way of life. My parents raised my brother, sister, and me to the best of their abilities and the values that they instilled in us. Who can say they have the perfect family? Although we had our ups and downs, I believed we came out all right. Just like any other family, we were normal people who have experienced things that tried to define who we were while we're here on earth. These things we carried down through the years and buried deep in our souls until something shook us out of our make-believe world of *talk no problem, see no problem, and speak no problem.* When you begin to see a glimmer of light, that is when hell broke loose and tried to draw you back down.

Yes, we were a normal family with issues and problems living life expectations of how a family should live, but how we endured through the life lesson was the key factor of how we would end up with the choices we made in our lifetime.

My views of love, pain, joy, and disappointment played a major role in my life as a young child. I did not have a clue that it would follow me into my adult life. One of the most important things that I held on to until this day besides the love of God is believing and knowing that my family loved me even when they did not always express it—even through the disagreements, the separations, the laughter, the pain, the sorrows, the noisy times, and the total silence. I understood that this was how a normal family would express themselves in how they viewed the surroundings of their life situations. I only saw the perfect family portrayed on television. When they made a mistake, the director would say, "Cut," and they would do a retake. However, there was no one to say, "Cut." We just expressed it in silence and allowed time to smooth things over.

As years went by, people around me began to change. The things that I began to focus on brought more questions to my mind. I wanted to understand why certain things were happening to me in my life. These changes would continue, and I did not have any idea of how I would be able to handle them. One significant thing I used to do was override the hurt and disappointment with my imagination. One childhood secret that worked well for me was my imagination. It helped cover me from the shadow that hovered over me from life disappointments. I believed it was the imagination of the beauty that God embedded deep in my mind, which brought warmth and security. This allowed me to see those who brought disappointments in my life as obstacles that I had to learn how to deal with when I faced them. Eventually, these persons became a vapor that slowly disappeared into thin air in my mind. I was just a child who saw things without definition, and things were just a simple way of living.

As I got older, the views of people in various situations seemed to linger longer and remained painted in my mind—especially when these images would not disappear but brought pain and hurt. The image of their faces would go away for a while but was never erased.

These images were of those you looked up to for guidance or in high positions—those who told you what to say and how to act. The consequences behind your response for not doing what they said were a high price to pay. You got a whipping, or worse, you felt like an outcast from family members and friends. I used to think the trials of my life disappointments were like a childhood game and that if I finally grew up, it would be over. That is what they call the game of life. The opponents in that arena did not play fair at *all*! I will explain that later in the book.

Even as an adult, I realized childhood games can become patterns we hold on to when making life choices. There are people who simply refuse to play by the rules in this world. So we hoped perhaps we would find a game that everyone played fair. This is the interesting part of life. When you play the game of life, your opponent's goal is to destroy you. Your chances of surviving are very slim.

Then when you find the one who not only can give life but also give life more abundantly, the views all around begin to come clearer of where you're headed on this life's journey. I have made progress in my growth in Christ, and it is much easier to see people through God's *eyes* than my own eyes. This was my pattern for many years—seeing the things around me from my eyes and point of view without fully understanding the source of what caused us to act and react to the things around us. This was a pattern that I adapted to and became so familiar with and carried over into my adult life; this pattern took me in many directions growing up from a little girl to a woman.

Little did I know or understand that each given day was an opportunity for me to capture the beauty that was embedded in my mind as a child by God. The beauty of hope and the realization that change would come with an understanding. I needed stability in knowing who I was and why I was born. This was a thought that grew as years went by in my life. The days turned into weeks, weeks into months, and the months into years. My life became more of a challenge in learning how to cope with different barriers that would come my way. My view of people and situations became different. I blamed it on everything that did not make sense to me at that time. I was no longer the little girl who saw things without definition or meaning. The thing that would bring peace and comfort seemed so far away. There was nothing close that gave me that inner feeling of security and comfort. The influences of things around me began to shape me into someone who was not the true me.

Yes, I was growing older, but the situations around me seemed to remain the same—situations that consisted of pain lingering longer and the harsh words that were hard to forget. However, I had no choice but to go with the flow. Deep down within myself, I searched for ways to ease the pain and bring comfort to my mind and heart. So I began to view the people in a very dull way—ways that I felt would help me to deal with them the best way that only I knew how.

Growing up, my sister and I would play make-believe every chance we got. That was the time when she and I would find ourselves in a world that would be exactly as we wanted it to be. This world took us to a place of comfort and fun. We had good parents with bad habits, and I believed that they raised us to the best of their ability. As a family, we shared the love and pain in our own way even though sometimes the pain was unbearable. The mishaps that came and went and the secrets no one volunteered to speak openly about remained just that—secrets. They remained secrets until time would allow them to be revealed. We were all people made up of families that expressed the trials and woes of living in a world designed on different views of life.

Opportunities may not knock on every door, but perhaps someone will open their door to get a peek and have a small measure of happiness. However, one had to be careful peeping in open doors because what seems right can be wrong. God knew the things that would harm my views on life. Yet God gave me the opportunity to capture the beauty that he laid within my mind that only a child could imagine. As I grew older, it faded away.

There were times when things were good, and I wanted those times to last forever. The reality of forever is not written in this world. But I am glad to know that there is forever, and I am determined to get there. This thought even brought an unawareness of an unknown darkness that would walk with me until I yielded to it. This unknown darkness lay dormant, like a snake watching its prey until it knew when to strike. I could only do what was allowed, and that was to live freely in a world of opportunities that consisted of good and evil.

Unfortunately, some of these opportunities kept me in a place where the darkness in my life continued. This became a place without definition or meaning—places that would teach me the best and the worst things as time went on. I sometimes found my mind traveling back to those places and wished they never took place. However, I have learned in life that the things people go through are truly for a reason. The hard part was that I did not know that it was going to be tough.

When I was a little girl, the things around me seemed to be so simple. It was defined as good. Things just made sense, and nothing was complicated at that time in my life. This was all that I knew to accept. These things were told to me by my parents, aunts, uncles, and other people who were older than and wiser than me. I believed that all of this would keep me in a safe place. This type of happiness would not tarnish my view, as I knew it.

Unfortunately, that was not true. Things that were built on uncertainties could easily crumble. These things made life seem to be more difficult than enjoyable. Although these events in my life were not always clear, it took time for me from a little girl's point of view to view it from a woman's point of view. I guess I was still not close to what I needed to shape my life. It was a long process to understand what was and what is, and what is to come that would define my life.

We are told that life is a process which consists of many situations and difficulties. God only knows, and I am glad that he does. However, I would find myself sitting and wondering over the things that had happened to me or why I chose to do the things I did. This was my time to see how many rounds I will go with self-pity. My life was not like the life of those I was watching on television. You put yourself in the ring and see how many rounds you can go. I wondered if I would ever find true happiness to make things better in my life. Although watching from the outside of other people's lives, I saw that theirs really seemed far better than mine. The older I got, the more I was exposed to different things. Normal was not meeting the status quo. I began to think, "What is normal?" Living in a world trying to understand what life really means and seeing how you are living just does not connect with every dot on the paper.

Yes, my family is typical, and the characteristics of each one of us brought a multitude of colors that displayed who we were. We lived the best that we knew how and tried to bring something positive into our lives when we could. In our house, there were rules and regulations. My father was the disciplinarian. He was a man who had a good heart. Many hard things that he grew up with followed him in our family, and we suffered for that. But there was no doubt in our minds the love my dad had for his family. However, when he was around, we were like little soldiers. All my mom had to say was, "I'm going to tell Lenard." That's my dad's name. We would immediately straighten up. Fear came over us all, and we knew enough that we did not want to get in Lenard's line of fire.

My mother was a comfort to us. She was the one who softened the encounters of our dad when we had to endure them. My mom is a person who loved the only way that she knew how—the way that she was loved by her parents. I learned that as I became a woman and God opened my eyes to see and understand her in a better way. She was a person who allowed a person to really get close to her heart, and then that person could probably get anything he or she wanted. But when they made her upset, they'd better watch out!

My brother was the oldest, and my sister was the youngest. Now you figure that one out. I was the middle child. No, I am crying, "Marsha, Marsha, Marsha," but I do understand Jan's point. Through it all, God has blessed me to know and understand my parents and my siblings, and all of us did what we only knew to do, but the love we had for one another was strong. There were times we would allow the weight of the problems, disappointments, and disagreements to shadow us; but it never could cause the love to be moved from us. When families feel pain and disappointment, it is when love can feel foreign. I give God the *praise* in our unknowing that he knows how to hold a family together through it all until we come together and utterly understand one another. My parents loved us the best they could. I can honestly say I will not trade them for anything in this world. This is 2024, and God has blessed my parents, my brother, and my sister to still be here among the living; and I am incredibly grateful. I know that each day is an opportunity to show them how much I love them with the love of God, a love that has brought completeness and understanding to see things as he sees them and endure one another with his love—a view to see them as God sees me and treating them with his love because everyone is incredibly special in his eyes.

SCHOOL DAYS

A Teen's View

I grew up in a small country town, in a neighborhood that was fun and exciting. My dad and mom rented a house from one of their friends who owned rental houses. You know back in the day, if you had houses for rent, you had clout in the neighborhood. It was like living near the Joneses.

Living in this rental house made the lady landlord and my mom become good friends. Until this day, they are remarkably close friends. She had four children, and we all played together every chance we got. The oldest daughter, whom I will call Friend A, and I attended the same schools together from first grade to the twelfth grade. As children growing up, we had our differences from grade school throughout high school. Regardless of what we faced down through the years, it did not tarnish our friendship. Today, I count it as gain because now I see it in a new perspective, different from that when I walked the path that was designed for my life.

My school days were typical times as a child, a teenager, and a young woman. Going through school, I encountered three people who played a significant part in my life as friends; and those three people were Friend A, Friend B, and Friend G. I will only use their first initials in their first name for privacy purposes. Although I had many friends during this time, it is just these three who altered my way of thinking in certain areas of my life. I believed it was God's intention for us to cross paths because of the lives each of us has endured through the years.

The first friend I remember was Friend A. We would play together almost every day until she got mad at me. We went to school together from first grade to high school. Some days, we would all hang out in the neighborhood with our other friends and enjoy the times we all had together, playing with each other all day long. Looking at it now, I see how each one of us had a role to play. Our friendship went through things for the better and the worst of times. Seeing it from a different perspective today, I am thankful for those times now. These life lessons that God blessed us all to endure have brought me to a good space with him today.

Regardless of the ups and downs as a child, teenager, and adult, we were like a family that had different opinions, and we grew up together the best way we knew how. I believe that our friendship brought a particular bond of respect. We will always be connected as a family of friends no matter what happens through the years. At the end of the day, that respect was real, and no matter how many life situations may have tried to bury that, it remains today. There can be so many things you gain throughout life. It takes God to bring it to the surface from beneath the rubble so you can use it at its appointed time. I give God the praise for that kind of love. This is a love that gets better as the days go on with the help of God on your side.

To share a little history about both families, I remember times when our families would come together, and we would have good times just hanging out. No one was perfect or better than anyone, although we could think that we were because we compared ourselves to one another based on the things that we had and what we faced in our families during that time. These types of views would cause jealousy, bitterness, and judgment that would leave a residue to follow us along the years toward one another. Views that caused you to hate and judge could dull your view in the long run. I have dealt with uncomfortable being excluded in your own family, but when that same thing begins to spread, it is like a forest fire. Relationships can be built on everything, and they can fall on anything if you do not have God in your life to bring balance. Only the *love* of God can bring stability to any relationship. His love is the key to forgiveness and understanding, first beginning within and then to those around you. You begin to see people as God sees them. This is how I see people today, not from the view that was built within me from a child, teenager, or young woman but a view as God has placed in me to see them with a heavenly sight. He has helped me to love, forgive, and pray for them just like my intercessor who sits on his right side and prays for me.

I believe Friend A is a leader. She always took charge of our small neighborhood girl pact. Our girl pact would get together; and whatever Friend A said, that is what we did. I know that we would say that Friend A was controlling, and that might be true. One thing was for sure, behind that controlling spirit she had, I still believe she was born to lead.

Now when you did not do what Friend A wanted, she would get the other girls to not talk to you, and you would be excluded from the group for weeks. They would form their own little clique. Guess who was the one being excluded from the group most of the time. Yes, you are right—it was me. The more it happened, the less I wanted to be a part of that group. You know how people say bad karma follows you? Well, that is what it felt like for years for me. I felt that something bad was following me. I just did not know what it was. The older I got, the more this type of behavior I had to face. I had to learn how to deal with it on my level. Come on, you know how it was when you wanted to be a part of the popular group and you were not! Imagine going through this dark cycle from elementary to high school. Well, I did, and I tell you it was not nice at all. I accepted it, and I made up my mind that I was not going to allow anyone to tell me whom to talk to or how to behave. If I had to be by myself, and many times I was, so be it. It was not easy, but it was a fact.

Yes, it is a cycle, but now I understand who was behind this cycle. This is 2024, and this darkness is yet alive and moving in the lives of those who do not know or understand the intent he has for their lives. I have seen this darkness which caused this behavior to be displayed in families, communities, and, sad to say, even in the church. I had no clue about this darkness growing up from a little girl to a young woman. Today I am aware, but I am not alone. Greater is *he* that is in me than he that is in the world.

Let me continue to share with you how this darkness continues to follow me and played a part in my life. When I was in grade school, I loved being around my friends and some of the teachers. I enjoyed learning, but most importantly, I love to make people laugh. I remember when they decided to close the schools where the Black children attended in 1968. This was the time when Black and White would come together in the small town called Lufkin, Texas. I was promoted to the third grade and about to attend a new school. I remember the first day my mom took us to Slack Elementary and enrolled my brother, my sister, and me. It was a different school, and we no longer looked the same. As the weeks went by, things seemed to flow okay. I met different people, but most of the Black children hung with the Black, and most of the White hung with the White children. One day in the classroom, this little White girl and I became friends. We would hang out at recess, and our desks were in the same area in the classroom.

I remember my third-grade teacher—I will never forget her name—Ms. Austin. She was not like my first-grade teacher Ms. Fondren, who was White. Ms. Fondren was nice, and she made you feel safe. Ms. Austin, on the other hand, was hard; and she looked at you with still cold eyes. As my friendship with Cindy grew, it did not matter how Ms. Austin looked at me. I had a friend, and it was okay.

One day, Cindy and I were sitting at our desks, and we were writing on this piece of paper. Cindy wrote a word that began with the letter *f*, and we both sat there, giggling because it was funny to us both. Then we heard a firm voice directed at both of us to come to the front of the class. It was Ms. Austin, and she said, "Bring that paper with you!" We both got up slowly and were so scared because we did not know what was about to happen. As we both stood in front of her, she took the paper and began to read the words that were written on the paper. Cindy began to cry, and Ms. Austin pointed out the word with the letter *f* and asked who wrote that word. I was speechless at the time; I could not open my mouth. I knew that Cindy wrote it, but I was so scared I stood there with my mouth closed tight. Then suddenly Cindy said, "She did it." With tears filling my eyes, I said, "No, I didn't. She did." Ms. Austin looked at me with hate in her eyes. It was a look that would kill. Of course, she believed Cindy and not me. She looked at me; and with a cold firm voice, she said, "Go back to your seat, and sit down, and don't you say anything more today." She did not say anything to Cindy, and we both headed back to our desk to sit down. But from that day forward, she never looked at me the same. Every time I found my eyes locked on hers, she gave me a hard look as if I had contaminated my friend Cindy. This was my first experience of prejudice because of the color of my skin. I had a feeling that is hard to shake when I look at certain movies or see certain things that relate to prejudices because of skin color. I thank God today that I realized that it was not Ms. Austin who was bad; it was the influence that drew her to believe that she was justified to feel the way she did. I dreaded facing the next teacher the following year because I did not know if I would experience the same look from year to year from White teachers. Fortunately, I did not experience it. I had wonderful teachers who had White skin, who treated me with warmth and kindness. They made me feel comfortable in their classroom until I finished grade school.

When I made it to the seventh grade, it seemed like time went by so fast. In a small town, you would think everybody knew everybody, but this is not true. Yes, we knew each other because we were in the small community and the same school from year to year, but I believed that the seventh grade was my best year. It was a time I felt independence from things that I felt were holding me down. I knew I was heading for a new beginning, and my classmates seem to be more mature and not childish. I believed that I was ready to begin a new path with some of my old and new friends. However, when things seemed good, darkness always tried to find a crack to creep in and cause havoc. Those whom I thought were my friends, our friendships were an on and off type kind of friendship because they were easily influenced by someone who had enough power to make them believe differently, and not strong enough to walk in what they believed to be true. It did not last. I experienced those types of encounters until I graduated from high school.

THROUGH THE EYES OF A SHEEP

Meanwhile, I endured seventh grade. There was one day when things began to look up for me. That was the day I met Friend B. She was tough and rough around the collar, as you would say. She did not take too much off anyone. Friend B and Friend A became enemies when we were in the seventh grade. Their relationship remained that way long after we graduated from high school.

They both had the same personality of taking charge and being in control. Friend B did not care for Friend A, and the feeling was mutual. They learned that they did not see eye to eye on certain things. Then I met Friend G. She and I connected in a way that we were more passive and wanted to get along with everybody. It was like we were pawns on a chessboard, and if we did not allow either of them to move us in the way they wanted to, then we were thrown off the board. However, we all had to learn to walk the path from seventh grade through high school together the best way we knew how.

We made it to junior high, and Friend B and I hung out every chance we got during and after school. We became close friends, and we shared one thing in common. We both loved gymnastics. By the time we reached the eighth grade, we were best friends. We would hang out after school and would take turns going over to each other's houses. We talked about being gymnasts when we got to high school. This was one of the most exciting times in my life. To think back on how excited I was, doing this together brought pleasure and laughter to my heart. We were inseparable in junior high school. We even made up our own language. Our daily routine after lunch was to go in front of the school and do flips and practice on our gymnast moves. That was our thing, eat lunch quickly and go outside in front of the schoolyard and show off how good we could do our flips. Although Friend B was better than me, watching her encouraged me to try harder.

Friend B was more like a protector to me. Nobody messed with her because she would fight for no reason. She did not take too much off anybody. One day, we were walking down the hallway to class. She had been wanting to fight Friend A ever since the seventh grade. As we continued to walk down the hallway, she leaned closer to me and whispered in my ear, "I'm going to bump into her so we can fight." In my mind, I thought a wall of nerves began to build up because I did not want to fight. I sure was hoping that she did not want me to help. As we both were approaching Friend A, my eyes connected with her, and I saw she was laughing and whispering in the ear of the person she was walking with. I heard Friend B say, "Here she comes," and she moved closer to her, but she had locked her arms with mine and pulled me with her. She bumped into her, and they started to fight. As the fight broke out, I ended up between them both. Well, the rest is history. The fight was on, and all three of us were led to the vice principal's office that day.

As we sat in the office waiting for the assistant principal to return, I was scared because back then, you got the board, and they called your parents later. I was thinking, "How did I end up in this mess?" It just proved that sometimes those you choose to walk with will lead you on a path that was not meant for you to follow. After being called into the principal's office, Friend A began blaming both Friend B and me for starting the fight. But Friend B, being the friend that she was toward me, told the vice principal I had nothing to do with it. I barely got off, but she was suspended for three days. But she didn't care because she felt she had accomplished what she wanted to do, and that was to fight the one girl that she had longed to fight for such a long time. Friend B had that type of mind-set that when she set her mind to something, she would pursue it to accomplish it. That is how she is today. God has blessed her life, and I am glad that our paths crossed. You will see why as you continue reading.

After the three-day suspension, Friend B returned; and as usual, every day after lunch, we would go in front of the schoolyard and do our flips. It seemed like everything was back on track. However, on this day, the vice principal was standing and looking at us for a long time. I felt that he wanted to say something to us, but I ignored his look and continued to do flips. He came over, and he began to talk to us. He stood there for a while, and he kept looking up at the sky. I found myself wondering, "Why is he looking up at the sky?" But I did not dare ask him what he was looking for.

Then as he began to speak, he seemed to focus on me, and he began to share what was on his mind. At that point, I felt like I knew without a shadow of a doubt what he was about to say. If you had asked me how I knew what he was going to say, I would have told you, "I do not know." However, it was just like someone dropped a thought into my mind. He came over, and he had a smile on his face. He stood there watching us as we did our flips. Then he looked up into the sky, and then he looked at me and asked me this question, "Are you going to be ready when Jesus comes back?" No one really answered, and I just looked with a slight smile on my face, thinking about his question. Like the others, I did not say anything. Really, I did not have an answer to his question. I did not even know much about Jesus or anything on his return. Friend B continued to do her flips, but I stood there quiet as his question continued to go over and over in my mind. I did not say much at that time. I just kept what I was feeling to myself and went to class. But that question stayed on my mind for the rest of the day. I did not have an answer, and that made my life a little more puzzling. I thought about what I knew he was going to say and why this particular question lingered with me. The only thing at that time I could think of was that I did not know how to find the answers to my questions.

 I made it to the eighth grade. Getting ready to have the time of my life was what I thought. That one question on that day kept surfacing every now and then. Will you be ready when Jesus comes? This was one question that I would try to forget and bury in the deepest part of my mind. I felt that I didn't have time to think about being ready when Jesus would come back, especially when I didn't know who he was. I continued to live my life as a normal teenager thinking that I had buried that question in the farthest part of my mind. I thought I did because just as it came, it left my mind the same way. It didn't actually leave me. I thought about the question every once in a while.

 The following year, Friend B became a cheerleader, but she had dropped out of school because she got married. I had mixed feelings. I was happy and sad for her. I felt like she was going on with her life and I was stuck in school. As we grew older and we grew apart, we did not spend much time together because her lifestyle had changed. She was married, starting a family as a mother and a wife at an incredibly young age. I was still looking forward to going to high school hoping the plans for my life would come through for me. Friend B and I did not see each other as much, but when we got a chance to see each other, we would cherish the times and then go our separate ways. We both grew older and began to go down our own paths in our lives. The relationship between me and Friend A was not quite the same since that fight. But our path continued to cross from junior high to high school.

Once we got to high school, you'd think that we had grown a little wiser and a little more mature. Unfortunately, this was not the case. People will continue to be who they are until true change occurs in their lives. I believe we are who we are until true change occurs in our lives by God, which can only be for the better. We are just who we are until that change happens.

I continued to experience the ups and downs of relationships between people during school. The cycle of darkness tried to dominate my life with this negative activity. This sometimes brought feelings of loneliness and not fitting in with the right group of people. You just do what you do, and some days will be better than others. But loneliness has a way of creeping up on you and will reside if you do not know how to evacuate it from our presence. That is when the challenge comes because everything around you that you see others doing is the norm. So you feel that you need to be doing the same thing with your own group or you need to be included so that you won't feel like an outcast.

You know when you grow up in a small town around the same people most of your life, you usually find yourself with our so-called friends who easily persuade us to do what they are doing. You set yourself up as a target because you are too weak to say no or you just do not know any better. As mentioned earlier, Friend A had the influence to lead people. She used that to dominate her group of friends, and when you did not follow, you were no longer a part of her group. I remember one day Friend G came to me. It was one of those isolated days of being cast out. I was feeling my lowest and trying to make it through the day until it was time to go home. Friend G met me in the hallway at the changing of the rooms. I was at my locker, and she came up to me. The words she said to me were so comforting. She informed me that the word that was going around that day with the group was not to talk to me. But she said she did not care what the others had been instructed to do, I was her friend, and she was not going to do what they were doing. I really needed to hear that. She lifted my spirit that day. She and I became the best of friends, and she will always hold a special part in my heart.

Today, Friends A, B, and G are all friends. I believed that we could look back and laugh at the times that we shared as young children to our womanhood. We can say that we know that it was by the *grace* of God that we were brought through trials as children from elementary school to high school and to adulthood.

My eyes see the quality that God instilled in Friend A and Friend B; they both were born to lead. They had the ability to influence and gravitate people to their presence. Sometimes, this could work to our advantage or disadvantage, depending on who we are following. There were several relationships that suffered setbacks because of my relationships with others while I was growing up. That is part of life, and it's all part of growing up; unfortunately, this dark cycle will follow you even when you are an adult.

Fortunately, God has allowed us to grow older and wiser to where I believe that we are set in places to lead in a more positive way, which leads to having a relationship with the Father, Son, and the Holy Spirit. As for the women who have been mentioned, I believe we can all say the following, "If it wasn't for God, I don't know where I'd be." I give God the praise that we are still friends to this day, and we can sit together and laugh over the things that we shared growing up as children. This is what I know to be true true today in 2024. I give God the praise, for he opened my eyes wider to see the precious traits from those he allowed in my path. I pray that God will draw them closer and that he will continue the purpose that he has designed for their lives.

It was December of 1974; I was in ninth grade, and it seemed like a pivotal point hit my life. Time was different and seemed like I was hearing more things about God, Jesus, and the world coming to an end. I was hearing several people in the community saying different things about when Jesus was coming back, which took me back to that day when the vice principal asked that question concerning Jesus's return. I would hear several people I knew who went to church faithfully saying that the world was coming to an end soon and when it would happen, Gabriel would blow his horn. There were some who indicated the year that it would happen, which was 1975. Now it's December of 1974. Can you imagine how I was feeling at this time? One thing for sure is I was not looking forward to the first day of the New Year of 1975. The fear in me rose, and I believed that it was going to happen. Fear is something especially when you do not know the facts about something or someone.

I did not go to church, and I didn't know much, but somehow my nerves were turned inside out, which caused the worst discomfort through my whole body at that time. I was hoping December 1974 would last forever because this was the hardest and scariest time for me. December 31, 1974, had come and gone. It was one of the worst days of my life. I was silent inside and out. Any day now, I was waiting for Gabriel to blow his horn. It was midnight as I watched TV, seeing the people who were happy and celebrating the New Year. When everyone was singing and saying, "Happy New Year!" I felt like I was walking on eggshells. I finally was able to go to sleep and woke up the next morning. Looking up at the sky wondering if the world was coming to an end that day was driving me crazy. I found myself watching Christian programs on television more and hearing the same familiar words about Jesus. Words that were not comforting but brought confusion to my mind. The words were just going over my head. Perhaps it was the fear that was overriding my thought process. I did not understand any of it. However, I found myself thinking more about what I thought I knew about God and Jesus, and the thoughts would not leave my mind even if I wanted them to. As days turned into weeks and weeks turned into months, it was nearly December. This brought an ease of release to my mind. The year 1975 was over, and now it was 1976, and I found myself thanking a God I did not know much about for not letting the world come to an end in 1975. I felt like I could breathe again and seemed like everything was back on track once again, and I was living my life as a fifteen-year-old teenager looking forward to becoming sixteen years old.

In 1977, one of my mother's sisters died of stomach cancer. It was one of the saddest times of my life. She was an aunt whom I loved to be around. She was cool. I felt free around her, and I loved the strength I felt when I was with her. I knew without a shadow of a doubt that she loved me. My parents were firm, especially my dad, and there was a certain way we had to behave around him. When I was with my aunt, she allowed me to be free and enjoy life as she knew it. My aunt was not crazy. She did not let me do drugs, but she would let me taste a wine cooler every now and then. She treated me like her little sister rather than her niece. I was sixteen years old, and she treated me like an adult with certain boundaries.

My aunt's health was failing that year in 1977. The last time I saw her was in her hospital room, and they were rolling her out to go take some x-rays. My family traveled to Houston that weekend to visit her in the hospital. We arrived in Houston early, and I stayed overnight with my aunt in the hospital. It was time to return home to Lufkin. My family came to the hospital before leaving to pick me up. I remember the day before we left, my aunt and her husband were having a talk. I was just sitting there listening. Then my aunt looked at me, and she stared at me with sadness in her eyes. I stared right back at her with a slight smile on my face without saying a word. All I could see was the pain on her face as she continued to look at me. Then she said to me, "I am sure glad I got to see you grow up because I won't see my children grow up." Hearing those words made me feel incredibly sad, and it brought tears to my eyes. I wanted to cry, but I could not, because I did not want her to see me crying. I was trying to be strong for her even though the little peace that I had was slowly drifting from my life at that very moment. I loved my aunt so dearly. She understood me, and she talked to me with love and warmth.

My mom and dad made it to the hospital, and we stayed there until it was time for us to leave. The door to her room opened, and a hospital worker came in and told my aunt that they were going to take her up for x-rays. Everybody exited out of the room, and I stayed at the bedroom door as they took my aunt up for x-rays. The last time I saw my aunt alive was when I stood at her hospital room door. I remember two people coming into her room to take her. I will never forget the look she had in her eyes as they rolled her by me. Our eyes connected as though we were saying goodbye to each other. My heart was heavy that night. There was a pain that I had no idea how to handle. I carried that heaviness for many years in my heart and mind while finding ways to bury it and keep it suppressed. This was just another added weight along with other burdens that would accumulate in my heart over the years.

As we gathered in the car headed back home to Lufkin, it seemed like one of the longest rides home I had ever experienced. All I could see in my mind as I sat in the backseat of the car were my aunt's eyes looking at me as they rolled her by. We arrived home hours later, and as we unloaded the car and got settled in, my dad asked me to go and get some chicken for dinner. My sister and I went to pick up some chicken. As we returned with the chicken, we entered the house. There was a stillness in the atmosphere, and I noticed my dad sitting on the couch, looking at the television with a sad look on his face. I looked in the kitchen, and my mom was crying standing over the stove. I went into the kitchen and asked her what was wrong; she told me that my aunt had died. My heart sank. The pain was unexplainable, and I felt myself traveling deeper into a path of darkness with no direction.

The days would pass, and my life became more complex, and nothing seemed right. I was just living day by day—living on false hope and temporary fun. There was nothing that seemed meaningful that could bring comfort to my life or my soul.

As the years continued, it was 1979. I finished high school and went to college for a semester, yet I felt like I was going nowhere fast. Something had to change, but I did not know when or how. So my routine for living was based on day-to-day events. I felt helpless. Anything or anyone who could bring a little comfort would do. I was just existing in a world that had no meaning to me. What I saw was bland and had no color. It seemed like only those who had kept getting more were the ones who were flourishing with everything they wanted in this world. Thoughts began to race through my mind, which led to self-pity and wantonness. I began to think about when change would come and how long I had to wait. Yet the saddest thing about that was I did not know who to turn to. I was surrounded by many people, but no one seemed to have the answer.

It may sound familiar, but life is a circle, and we all experience something that others can relate to. When you find yourself in a place of the unknowing, that is when your life feels like all uncertainty hits you in the face for the very first time. This was a time when things in my life seemed like it was out of control. I had a few friends and more associates than needed. I began to hear more about Jesus and God once again, which seemed to bring more confusion than answers. There were several people who would come up to me and say religious things. I didn't understand it at this stage of my life, and I didn't know what it all meant. It was like, if God was trying to tell me something, I wish it would have been a little bit clearer. To me, it was just people coming to me, saying religious things. But when I heard these things, it made me afraid, and I would try to close it out of my mind quickly. I did not want to hear about them, because I did not know if it was true or real.

Today, I know that God was trying to tell me something, but he had to bring me out of my mess to place me on clear ground so I could receive it. Living in my twenties, I felt the child in me was vanishing slowly, and the path for my life began to unravel in many undesirable ways. Things that I desired did not come as easy as I thought they would. I was raised in a house where we were not made to go to church. My family did not talk about God or Jesus that much, so I thought we just make the best out of life. Boy, was I wrong! How could one make the best of something when one did not know what the best was? As the years went by, I lived the path of my life from a young girl, to a teenager, and to a young lady dragging along the problems of my family and others around me. They didn't consume me, but they really contaminated my thoughts and thinking process that caused me to make wrong choices in my life. I was going somewhere, but for sure I did not know where I was headed.

As years went by, things began to change in my life. Thoughts were just racing in my head. Thoughts that were pulling me in directions that I was fighting to go. Sometimes, I would find myself afraid to lie down and go to sleep because I thought it would be over. I was taunted by nightmares of darkness that I did not understand. I did not have anyone to talk to about my experiences, and then I felt like, "Who would believe me?" All I knew was that this darkness brought more fear than anything—a darkness that had been following me all my life and made itself known to me since I was a young child, a darkness that would continue to follow and intimidate me until it could not any longer.

All I wanted was to have what I thought I saw other families around me have—families that seemed to have a little piece of true happiness. This was the view my eyes saw from the outside. However, when I got a chance to visit inside these homes, I realized that some of them were no different from mine. I found out that they, too, had a bit of dysfunction. I found it sad to say, but that brought a little comfort to my mind but no peace. Families with the nicest members were the ones who were crying out for help the loudest. Unfortunately, it was a cry of silence.

It is easy to take the positive events of our childhood and apply them to our adult lives without understanding the core meaning of those events. I found myself saying, "I did it because my mom did it (or my dad did it)," just to bring justification to the choices I made. But my actions brought consequences and affected not only me but also those who surrounded me. However, the things we do really start from our childhood. What if we do not have the kind of house our friends have or the fine cars and fashionable clothes? Does that really define who I was created to be by God? No, it only allowed the enemy to place more negative thoughts in my mind that I was not good enough or I did not deserve it, because I did not have them at the time I wanted them. I believe all these things are good. Most importantly now I know that, even though we didn't have the fine house, the best car, and fashionable clothes, I realized the importance of a house is to make sure your children can call it home and feel the love that will set the foundation for them to find the courage to believe that they can get from point A to Z and accomplish what is destined for their lives with the help of God.

I know that material things may bring comfort, but it does not bring stability of understanding of one life and the purpose of it. Family is more important than material things. That is something I learned as a child. These things can be goal driven, but once you have obtained these things and still find yourself in a place of unhappiness, then one must ask oneself, "What was obtained? Could it be something that needs repairing or needs replacing that was accumulated over the years?"

I realized now that my parents did their best from what was instilled in their lives as children from their parents or those who were responsible for raising them. I believed the only thing my parents ever wanted to do was to love us and make sure that we had a place to call home. Yes, we had our share of problems. My mom endured pain that I said I would not. I consider her to be a strong woman in her own rights. But even in her weakness, a glimmer of her strength shined through her struggles. Spousal abuse is an ordeal I do not wish on anyone. My mom had friends who would talk to her about her ordeal, but when it was over, no one really interfered with other people's problems. I believe that God gave my mother the strength to endure not because he wanted her to stay in that situation but because he knew that she did not have any other intervention to turn to. My dad is a strong man, who lived to make sure that his children had what he did not have as a child. He was a man who longed for his mother's love and a father who was not willing to show him love. He loved his father and did anything to make sure that he was taken care of. Although his father was abusive, those generation curses continue to follow and pour over into our little home.

In the relationship between my parents, I realized that two wrongs can only make matters worse; therefore, you must find the true solution to make it right. I believe the solution was God, who was absent from our lives down through the years. Hearing about him and having a relationship with him are two different things. I know without a shadow of a doubt that God can make any problem right when the parties involved want it to be right.

Looking at my parents' relationship, I made up my mind what things I would allow in a relationship with a man. I am sure not going to stay in situations that will bring more pain; at least that is what I put in my head. Yet, I realized that each generation is different and people dealt with the same problems differently. Families refused to talk about their issues openly because they felt it would bring shame and hurt, and perhaps open old wounds that have never healed.

One thing about knowledge is that you learn that there is nothing new that someone has gone through or will go through that has not been done before. I have learned that in life. I refused to let it be repeated in the lives of my children or their children. We can only live to the best of our abilities until we learn differently. Once we are better, then we should do better. As the word of God states, Jesus came that we may have life and have it more abundantly. I do not believe we were born to only exist to endure pain and heartaches until we die.

I was raised in a two-bedroom house for most of my life and bathed in a tin tub and had to heat water on the stove when taking a bath or washing dishes. I allowed myself to think repeatedly, "Could it have been better?" The answer could be yes, perhaps if I was born to other parents, but God designed my parents, and they did the best they could. As a child, a teenager, and a young adult, I wished we could have better things. Now as a young woman, if God gives me the ability to do better, then that is a choice I have to make, and I should not look for excuses about why the better does not come when I want it to come. I must just believe and keep my faith because of the relationship that I have with my Heavenly Father, my Savior Jesus Christ, and the Holy Spirit. We will always have a will to choose. People let reasons to cause them not to do what God has enabled them to do, simply because they refuse to follow the directions God has planned for their lives. But, first, they must understand and know the directions that God has for them to walk that path. Sometimes, we use reasons because we feel that those around us do not matter or we are not happy with ourselves.

Each day, the Lord has blessed me to understand better as I have gotten older. I had enough things that have happened in my life that could be used in a negative way. Therefore, I know that each situation that I have gone through will or has played a major part in my life today.

I believe and understand my life enough to know that there is someone higher than me. I did not know during this time in my life. In the '80s, I felt I was living my life as I wanted, did not have to answer to many people, and did what I wanted to do and who I wanted to do it with. The only sure thing in my life was my family and a few friends. I would watch movies and listen to songs to add to an imaginary world of comfort from time to time. Now let us not get it twisted; I was not delusional. It was just my method of finding a kind of peace in a time of confusion. This was just a way to escape from the reality of things that were occurring in my life, which I did not want to face at certain times. I was grounded enough not to let my imagination go too far. This was the child in me that gave me the ability to be free. That brought ease to my mind.

I believed that some people planned their lives based on what they see on television, what they hear people sing about, or an imagination that allows them to design a world that would bring comfort that will take away the pain and disappointments that occur in their lives. My imagination was a place I designed for myself and only myself. I just had to find the path that would bring order to my life. It had to be someone other than myself who could lead me to that point. I had many questions, but the most important question I would ask repeatedly was, "When will I understand my life?"

Being nineteen years old and not knowing much but thinking, I felt that I was an adult so no one could tell me anything. Are we really like sheep with nearsighted vision and unable to see far off? As God blessed me to see each new day of my life, the answer to that question would come eventually. When facing those I thought were my friends, I realized that our relationships were more on an associate's status. Then, having to deal with certain family members who thought they were better than you and your family, was a hard pill to swallow. The battle of trying to understand my life became a daily ritual and a competition within my mind. It seemed like when I was about to head straight for the easy street, well, there was a cliffhanger at the end of the road. Only God knew the different incidents that went on in my life. Those events were no joke; some were life-and-death situations.

These incidents made me feel happy, sad, used, abused, or I just did not belong in this world. Only God knew who would help me to understand the choices that I had made and the choice I was going to make that would lead me in the direction toward the path he had designed for my life.

Understanding my parents and their relationship, I thank God for helping me to put that in perspective, allowing me to be there for them no matter what. My parents took me as far as they could, but God had someone else in mind to reach me with a deeper depth in him. He knew that I needed a spiritual connection that would bring me to the most important relationships that I would ever encounter on this earth. I wanted to obtain a relationship with my heavenly Father that would bring understanding and meaning to my life with him. I remember praying to God one night while sitting on my father's car. I asked God this question from my heart: "God, before it is all over, please let me get to know who you really are." I believed in my mind and heart someone heard my plea that night, because that night, I felt a warmth that I had never experienced before. It felt like someone had placed a warm blanket around me and was embracing me. What I had asked him was all I knew how to ask. Those words came from my heart.

After that night, I would continue to do as I would usually do living my life as usual doing what I knew best. Each day seemed the same. I would lie down to sleep and rise the next day. I began doing the same thing repeatedly, with questions of uncertainty that hung inside of my head for many years. My family celebrated Christmas and Easter. Christmas was a time we received presents and heard songs about a baby named Jesus and Santa Claus. Easter was a time to get new clothes and dyed Easter eggs and watch a show on television about a man carrying a cross.

As the years went by, I really did not understand the connection between the two events. We were not made to watch these events on television. Yet we learned to respect it. Years went by, and I began to hear things that really did not make sense to me—things like Jesus died for sinners. I asked myself, "What is a sinner?" I did not know that I was one. I was having a good time. To me, there were bad people and good people. I was in a place of my own and felt that I was in the category of the good people. So this place brought pleasure, and I was comfortable in my skin. I found myself doing things that brought comfort and opportunities, which led to undesirable outcomes that affected my life in ways that weren't right. These things were very pleasing to my flesh but killing my soul.

It made me feel like I belonged, and nothing else really mattered. If I was sad, I would get high. If I was lonely, I would get high. If I was depressed—well, you know the story—I would get high. You might be wondering, exactly what did I do? Well, let me say this: it was enough to give me a one-way ticket to hell if I had left this earth without the Lord Jesus in my life, and not had a true relationship with my Heavenly Father.

I was living my life as a true sinner, I was dying spiritually, and my soul was sinking fast. I was lost in a place filled with darkness and shame. It was like my mind was in a race with my thoughts. The more it seemed like I needed to change, the more I found myself wanting to have a good time and trying to keep my mind occupied with something other than "Jesus came to save sinners." I once tried to convince myself that I would not be the only one in hell. At this point of my life, I thought that if I died, I would end up in hell together with the same people who were making my life miserable here on earth. Then I thought, did I really want to be in hell with them? And not thinking clearly, did I want to be in hell?

Knowing what I know now, Lord, I give you *praise*, for you have given me the understanding that hell is not a pleasurable or a social place where we will be able to converse with one another. There had to be a better way out, and only God knew how to get me there.

THE INVITATION

A Sinner's View

Several years had passed, and out of the blue one night, Friend B showed up at my door. She was different. She was not the same. She was incredibly happy and excited. She told me that she had accepted Jesus Christ as her personal Savior and she was saved, sanctified, and filled with the Holy Ghost. Lord, I did not know what in the world she was talking about.

As a little girl, I remembered my mother talking about the sanctified quarters in her hometown of Nacogdoches, Texas—how sanctified girls were different and how those who did not wear makeup or pants could not do anything but go to church. That was out of the question for me. I did not want to do that or be that. She said they were people who went to church a lot and felt the Holy Ghost. She said they were sanctified.

Well, now Friend B had told me she was sanctified and she no longer did the things that she once did. She said that she found the Lord, and it seemed like she was trying to convince me to find him on that night too. I knew that was not happening, but she did something that night that utterly convinced me that she had changed. Friend A lived one house from my house. For years since that fight in the eighth grade, they were enemies and had not spoken to each other. I knew without a doubt that Friend B hated her with a passion. She went over to Friend A's house that night and asked her to forgive her for all the things that she had done to her. She then came back to my house with that smile on her face and a sense of peace that covered her. I knew something was different, but I did not want to have anything to do with it at that moment. Because I had become comfortable in my skin and I did not want to change. So I smiled with her and talked with her for a while, and she went on her way—not knowing that she would be like an unwanted insect who would keep bothering me. She began to come over, continually knocking on my door for days to come. She was like a hound dog sniffing out sinners.

However, my attitude did not change right away, with the many attempts she made in witnessing to me about the Lord Jesus Christ. I remember one day I saw Friend B pulling up in the driveway. I told my mom to tell her that I was asleep. She came to the door and entered the house. My mother was in the living room. Friend B came in, and my mom told her that I was sleeping in my room. I pretended to be asleep on my bed. She came into my bedroom and shook me several times, and I lay there like a rock.

She then told me to get up because she knew I was not asleep. I was unable to lie still any longer and began to laugh, and she started her conversation as usual, talking about the Lord Jesus. Yet all the while as she was talking, I really was not giving her my full attention. Then the words I longed to hear flowed out of her mouth, "Well, I guess I will be talking to you later." I said okay, and she left.

Friend B was persistent, and she did not give up. I guess I should have known that about her because of the way she acted in junior high school. When she put something in her mind to do, she did it, just like that day in the hallway at school when she decided that she was going to bump into Friend A and started that fight. I guess she had the same mind about the devil. She was going to bump into him and fight and get sinners saved. I realized now that Friend B was the first important element in my life here on earth. She was used by God to lead me in the direction toward him so that I may know the plans he has for me on this earth. I am glad that Friend B was the tool God used to get my attention because she was not going to give up until she accomplished the task. God knew this, and I give him *PRAISE!* I believe God plans certain people for certain lives so that all lives will have a chance to get closer to him.

Then one day, Friend B came by and asked me to go to Ray's Drive Inn. Anybody who lived in Lufkin knew not to turn down an invite to Ray's Drive Inn. It was the best place to get a burger. The only reason I got into her car was I had a chance to get a hamburger basket from Ray's. I had made up my mind to ignore everything that she was going to say about Jesus. My plan was to tune her out when she mentioned anything that related to Jesus. We made it to Ray's, and I ordered a hamburger basket, and so did she. We sat there in her car, eating our food. Then Friend B began to talk as I ate my burger. There was a change in the atmosphere when she spoke. This time, she had my ear, and our conversation was different. Something about her words hit my heart. She said that Jesus would take away all the pain and hurt I was feeling so that I could be free.

I remembered that I had a lump of food in my mouth, and it was hard to swallow. She told me that Jesus loved me and, whenever I needed someone, he would be there for me. For the first time, I found myself really listening to her. The words were not bouncing off my ear; they were landing on my heart. The key words that captured my attention were *pain*, *hurt*, *free*, and *love*. These words went deep within me like someone had opened a floodgate. I still tried to eat my hamburger and not try to show any emotions. The tears began to flow out like water running from a faucet. I remember telling her that I did not know why I was crying, and she said to me that Jesus had touched my heart. It was one of the most remarkable feelings I had ever experienced in my life. It felt like the warm blanket that night as I sat on my dad's car, asking God that question. It was all over me, and everything felt like it was going to be all right for the first time in my life.

The feeling was amazing. It was not like I was feeling as though something, or someone, had dragged me through a muddy pit and I couldn't get out. You sit there hoping that you will not get caught and be punished knowing you needed help. Then someone comes and gives you a way of escape. You feel relief from the pain and hurt. The feeling in her car was the same feeling that I felt when I was sitting on my dad's car, but it was more intense and wonderful. It was an awesome feeling. I will never forget that day at Ray's Drive Inn.

That was the day God planted a seed in my heart to be cultivated with his love.

This was the first time in my life that I experienced the presence of God in that way—a presence that gave me assurance that no matter what I did not know, he would cover me all the days of my life. It was God who gave his Son, Jesus Christ, and the Holy Spirit, who covered me with their love and protection. I could not say anything. I could not eat anymore. The tears continued to fall. I knew I needed that peace and love that made me feel true happiness and freedom from Jesus. I cried over the rest of my hamburger basket that day. I cannot even remember if I completed the hamburger, but I do know from that day forward, our conversation was never the same.

When Friend B would come over, I wanted to hear what she had to say because it brought ease to a troubled mind. Then just as it began, it stopped. She didn't come over as much after that, and I didn't see her for a very long time. It was like space crept in between us, and it seemed like God allowed her to be distant from me for some reason. I will never forget that day at Ray's Drive Inn, and as I think back, that is when things in my life truly began to change without me knowing it. I would find myself going back to my routine, but there was a difference, and nothing would be the same afterward. Something had been planted within me that could not be taken away or stolen.

It did not stop me from experiencing what I thought were the best days of my life by satisfying myself with the pleasure of sins. I was a young woman, and I was determined to have fun. I loved going to the disco clubs and playing softball and hanging out with friends, drinking our wine coolers. Softball was the number one thing that consumed my time.

It was the summer of 1981, and I was playing a softball game with my team. We were having a good time. I was on third base, and the next batter came up to bat the ball. I remember running toward home plate. As I made it to home plate, a sharp pain hit the inside of my stomach. I thought the pain would leave, so I lay down on the ground, but the pain continued to get worse. Some of the team members took me home. I lay down once I got home. I tried to think that the pain would go away. The pain got worse, and my mother took me to the emergency room. They admitted me into the hospital. I was diagnosed with a bad kidney infection, and I remained in the hospital for five days.

My family came to visit and a few friends, but when they left, I was in that room by myself with the quietness. The pain was bad for several days, so I could not move around much. I had to remain still in bed. My mind was not clear to think of anything but the pain. As the days went by, the pain began to ease up and go away. I began thinking about my conversation with Friend B at Ray's Drive Inn. I could not do anything but think, and this was only day two.

I found myself wanting to see and talk to her, but I did not have a number to get in touch with her. Now the shoe was on the other foot. I wanted to see her, but I could not get in touch with her. I remember saying, "Lord, if you give me another chance to see Friend B, I will go to church." Just as I completed that sentence, her sister opened my hospital door. She worked there as a nurse's aide. I was so happy to see her. I asked her to have Friend B come to the hospital.

When Friend B got the message, she came right away, and we talked for a while, and I asked her about her church. She was happy to give me information about her pastor and wife and the church. Friend B called her pastor's wife on the phone, and I spoke with her briefly. She seemed to be a sweet person, and she invited me to come out to the church. I told her I would come.

When I got out of the hospital, I did not go right away, but I did eventually. I visited several times before I made up my mind to join. It seemed like for the first time I was in a place that showed light in the midst of the darkness in my life. Little did I know or understood the spiritual darkness that hovered over me as a child and an adult. This darkness did not want me to get closer to God. I had begun to learn and understand more about the word of God. However, I had a long journey to go and many things to learn, but I believed in the word of God and that everything would be all right.

My eyes were beginning to open, and my view was becoming clearer. I did not worry about viewing greener pastures. It was like my eyes were being focused on a direction that would bring me clarity and understanding—places that I thought would give me the fulfillment that I longed for down through the years. I was about to learn about someone who loved me so much that he gave his only begotten Son for my sins—someone who allowed his precious Holy Spirit to look at my every move when I did not know any better. All I had to do was to trust the Holy Spirit to lead me safely on the path designed for me by my Heavenly Father.

Even in a place of peace and warmth, darkness still tries to creep in, but these are things that we learned along the way with the help of a good shepherd, Jesus Christ, who is in heaven. There are earthly shepherds who are called and chosen by God to look out for his sheep here on earth. Becoming one of God's sheep is incredibly challenging, bringing about challenges that bring difficulties and changes every day. I was not alone, and I was not confused about the path that I was on now. I know that this challenge was a challenge worth taking. Now I understand why it is important to view things spiritually from the eyes as one of God's sheep. You must keep your eyes on God and the Lord Jesus Christ to understand your path, and you will understand the path that the Holy Spirit will lead you to.

INVITATION ACCEPTED

A New Beginning

It was 1981, and the path of my life had changed for the better. I had accepted Jesus Christ as my Lord and Savior, and I was striving to please him and my Heavenly Father. I went to church faithfully and attended Bible training for the new Christian, which we were then known as "babes in Christ." My old friend grew distant. Sometimes, certain family members did not understand why I was going to church like I was and why I was reading the Bible every chance that I got.

    Some days, I would find myself closed in my room just reading the New Testament. It felt like I was hearing Jesus speak to me through the pages of the Bible. He was filling his words in my heart with his love and understanding. It felt like I belonged to something that mattered in this world. I remember the first time I went to church, and I heard the pastor of the church preaching. I found myself sitting on the last pew in the back of the church just listening. The words that flowed from his mouth were words that found me in the deepest parts of my sin. At first, I thought he had been talking to someone about me, but I realized that I had not shared my secrets with anyone. It had to have been God that showed him my identity. He was just God's mouthpiece to lead the sheep. I continued to go, and I soon became a member. It was a little white wooden church on Cain Street in Lufkin, Texas. The members were few, but it felt like we were large in number because of the love of God that flowed within the church.

I believed that the people were truly genuine, and the word of God was preached and taught. After being there for several months, I believed that my pastor and wife were two of God's most beautiful people and they nurtured us with the love and compassion as God described in the scriptures. Until this day, they exemplify that love as they did the first day I met them.

That was over forty years ago, and I will continue to seek guidance from them because I believe they are truly spiritual leaders chosen by God. I have been under several spiritual leaders, and they poured into my life and gave my life substance. I believe everything, big or small, that comes from God is priceless. Regardless of what I faced in my life, a seed was planted and watered that will never be uprooted. That seed was the word of God, and it brought strength into my life and has kept the darkness from overtaking me.

My life was different, and I believed that I was on the right path and was headed in the right direction. I thought I had it hard when I was living my life without Christ. It really got hard when I decided to live for him. When I say hard, I do not mean it was hard living for him as a believer. The scripture tells us that the ways of a transgressor are hard. However, it was the devil and the work of his darkness that were used to throw foul balls every way that he could to throw me offtrack. I thank God for those who taught the new Christians in the church. We would have Bible study and drills to learn the tricky ways of the devil. The devil's job was and still is to deceive those who attempt to walk for God. As Jesus said in John 10:10 (KJV), "The thief cometh not, but for to steal, and to kill, and to destroy. I am come that they might have life, and that they might have it more abundantly." One thing for sure is when you learn who's the real enemy, your view changes on how you see everything around you. But it is a process and will take a spiritual leader who is really hearing from God.

I was a faithful member and attended services when the doors were open. I was taught how to fast and pray, and we did it according to the scriptures. The technique of learning how to fast and pray and seeking God was a challenge to the flesh, but I wanted to be filled with the Holy Ghost and the righteousness of God. I remembered hearing the pastor say that we should anoint our heads with oil and wash our faces and keep our minds on the Lord as much as possible.

I wanted it so bad even without knowing the steps to take. I went to the store and brought a bottle of olive oil and put some on my head before beginning a fast. I noticed that the hunger pains were still there. I thought this is not working because I am still hungry. As I grew in maturity, I learned that the oil was just symbolic of God's anointing and obedience in doing as Jesus instructed. It did not take the hunger away; it remained until I ate something. However, I learned about denying myself and being hungry for the righteousness of God. I wanted to abide in him and he in me, so I could be his faithful servant. This helped me to learn about self-discipline. As I learned that God had a plan for my life. I also learned that the devil had a plan too. To kill, steal, and destroy everything that God has designated for my life during my time here on earth. But I was just a babe in Christ just excited and naïve thinking everything will go smoothly since I decided to walk for the Lord. When I began this walk, I thought it was going to be quite easy and all my problems would go away. This was a tough lesson to learn but a lesson worth learning. One thing I do know is that it is very important to stay focused and listen to Spirit-led pastors who are after God's heart, and spiritual leaders who may be under them that are led by the Holy Spirit.

I believe as a new Christian, one must grow and go through stages before reaching maturity, just like a baby born into this world. Dysfunctional homes can curb the growth or even bring death to a baby. A dysfunctional church can do the same. The stages are critical, and spiritual leaders must be prepared and insured in God's will in knowing how to help God's children. They can develop and mature spiritually in knowing how to have a relationship with the Father, Son, and the Holy Spirit, and how to stand in a time of darkness. A new Christian is just like a newborn baby coming into a world, except we are coming into God's world, which is spiritual.

This world is totally different from the world that we have chosen to give up.

Spiritual leaders must be strong and in tune with God to make sure that new Christians develop five spiritual senses and use them just as the five natural senses. The five natural senses are sight, hearing, taste, smell, and feel. They determine our steps in making daily decisions. This applies the same way spiritually. The five spiritual senses are faith, love, understanding, wisdom, and knowledge that come from God. Without them, it would be difficult to walk the path that God has for us as believers.

The Holy Spirit is leading me on my path to be with my heavenly Father and my Lord and Savior Jesus Christ. Only the Holy Spirit can help me see things spiritually. This is how my spiritual eyes are opened as the eyes of a sheep. Hebrew 11:1 (KJV) says, "Now faith is the substance of things hoped for, the evidence of things not seen." Therefore, as a sheep, I can't view the things around me with my natural vision, because it could bring deception. It's what God wants me to focus on spiritually. There are things you cannot look at, touch, smell, taste, and hear with your natural senses on this walk with God because it can lead you back into the darkness. I learned the hard way about how vital it was to remain close to strong spiritual leaders and spiritual people until you are matured in God by the Holy Spirit. The word of God taught by my spiritual leaders helped me to understand the tricks and wiles of the devil. During this time in my life, the spiritual leaders in the church wanted us to take hold of understanding how to allow God to lead and direct our lives by his Spirit. We could receive every blessing that God had for our lives through this process. We could be effective and fulfill God's divine purpose for our lives. I still believe that what remains the same today is for every believer to achieve God's divine purpose for our lives.

Like a new child who was tempted with a lollipop, the devil and his cohorts made sure they played their role in my life, especially now since I began my walk with the Lord. Only this time, he came in a way that I least expected and had no clue of who he was because I did not know his ways fully or his intent. He came quickly, and he did not hesitate.

Reading the word of God over the years has brought consolation to my life. I did not know or understood the meaning of spiritual warfare in my early walk with the *Lord*, but I know it now. The day I accepted the Lord Jesus Christ and invited him to come into my life, the war took another direction because now I was standing on God's ground, and Satan didn't want me to know how much havoc we as believers can wreak on his territory.

The devil is not worried about how a person lives his or her life without Jesus Christ. He has them where he wants them. It is when you decide to give your life to God, and accept Jesus into your heart is when he really gets busy. I was naïve to think that when I began to live my life for God, everything was going to be like a bed of roses without the thorn. The fact is, the day I surrendered my heart to God, it was the day hell showed up at my front door disguised as the invisible man.

THE JOURNEY CONTINUES

A Sheep's View

My first year as a Christian was not so great. Temptation came in every direction. I was single and young. I went to work, church, and back home. These things were not bad, but it was not who I was in Christ. I realized and believed being under strong biblical teachings and strong leaders were essential in my daily walk with God. Romans 10:14 (KJV) says, "How then shall they call on him in whom they have not believed? And how shall they believe in him of whom they have not heard? And how shall they hear without a preacher?" There are steps in developing a person in their growth in Christ. Not only should a person be taught how to maintain one's life in God, but also be taught who they are in God to understand the position that God has placed them in for spiritual warfare and purpose.

My vision was weak to truly focus on the things of God at the beginning of my Christian walk. I was seeing things from a natural point of view. I believed in what my leaders were telling me at the time. It was not that I did not trust them, because I did. Hearing, listening, and not doing anything are three different things. Time went by, and I continued the same steps going to the altar seeking God and the Holy Ghost. This was all good at the beginning, but things began to change. It seemed like the Holy Ghost was not coming, and I could not be filled.

The devil began to play his hand by putting thoughts back into my mind, and I was visualizing the things that brought pleasure to my flesh and that will kill my soul. When I was around the saints, I had strength, and I felt fine. When I would be around those who could care less about the things of God, it caused my mind to wander. I would continually go to the altar crying and praying to God to fill me with the Holy Ghost. Every time I walked away without the evidence of speaking in tongues, my soul was heavy. It felt like something was holding me back. I did not understand what it was. I had accepted Jesus Christ as my personal Savior, but I needed the Holy Ghost. This was how I was taught. I would get so emotional and cry, which made me feel a little better, but it did not change my situation. It seemed like the effect was taking place on the outside and not the inside. I would go and shut in at church with other members, and we would stay there for days, fasting and praying unto the Lord for spiritual fulfillment. God blessed us because of our obedience in seeking him. We could only go on what we are taught by our leaders. My leaders passed on what had been taught to them from their spiritual leaders. All is good if it is going to lead you closer to God, but the question I would ask leaders today is, What destination point are you trying to reach in God, or is this a continuous journey? I believe there are leaders who will lead you the way they have been led. However, it is a blessing if your leader is spiritual and leading you the way of God's word by Holy Spirit. Therefore, my time with them was that time that God allowed, and I thank him for allowing that experience in my life.

I knew as a new believer I did not know that what I was being taught about God, Jesus, and the Holy Spirit was true. I had to trust that it was, and I continued reading and believing in God's word.

All I knew was that I wanted the Holy Ghost so badly that I was willing to do whatever it took to get him. I thought I understood what it meant to surrender unto the Lord. I felt that the only important thing was to allow him to do whatever he wanted in my life. Truly surrendering to God was an important process that I needed to understand. My desire was to seek and please God—to live my life the best I knew how according to his word. I tried to get closer to God and make one step closer. The devil would make sure something would pop in the way so I could make two steps backward.

Remember the saying "What goes up must come down"? Well, my life was up, and I was excited about finding God and the meaning of living as a true Christian. Even in the ways of a Christian, some of us take our eyes off the path and land in holes. There are some who are blessed to recover from the hole, and there are some who fall deeper into it and never recover. Living a Christian life for nearly eighteen months trying to hold on to what I have been taught was more than just speaking it. A drastic turn in my Christian life shifted toward the worst. I was fighting a continuous battle with my mind wandering back into the ways of the world from where God was bringing me out. I found myself thinking about those familiar things that pleased my flesh. I just did not want the familiar pain and loneliness that came with it. Things began to happen one after another—things that would change my walk with the Lord in a drastic way that brought shame.

It was in early 1983, and I was no longer identified as a Christian. I was officially a backslider. I felt like I was a black ball. I felt worthless, and what right did I have to ask God for anything? I remember that I wanted to go back to church and face the music and confess my sins, but I was too weak. If I knew my heavenly Father like I know him today, I would not have hesitated for so long to go back or given it a second thought. I would have found myself running back as fast as I could into his open presence of love.

Many unfortunate things began to occur in my life. Things that were not pleasant or pleasing to God or me. In my weakness, I realized that I was hurting God, my Lord Jesus Christ, and myself. It was at a period when I could not forgive myself. I decided not to go back to church altogether because I believed if I was going to live for God, then I would live for God; if I was going to end up in hell, then I would go straight there. This saying is stupid to someone who knows better, but when you are in a weak place, only God brings you out. Hey, you say and do stupid things! At that time, hell seemed like the only and right place for me. I was too weak, and I felt like this would be the right punishment for my actions. Praise God, he does not listen to us when we waddle in self-pity and say some of the dumbest things!

I learned that once you go back to the place where God has brought you out, you will never gain the peace that you once had with God until you return to him fully. I tried to find anything to keep my mind off the things of God, but this only worked for a while. The only thing I found myself trying to do was drown my thoughts in self-pity, and anything that would keep me focused on self-pity I would welcome it. The more people I hung around, the better it was. When I was alone, things were hectic in my mind and heart. Just as I was busy trying to forget, the devil was extra busy trying to dig a grave for my life.

I worked the night shift from 11:00 p.m. to 7:00 a.m., so I would sleep during the day and find myself just staying in my apartment. My days and nights were the same most of the time. When I was off from work, I would sit in my apartment feeling down and miserable. Then one day, I received visitors from the church that I was attending. They explained to me that someone had been harassing another member and her family with notes and letters. They informed me that they were informed that I was the one who was doing this. They asked me if I was the one who had been sending the notes to this member and her family. I looked at them and told them no. They talked a little while longer, but I was not really listening, because I was shocked. Why would they think I would do such a thing? Was it because I was a backslider and no longer in the church? Did they really think I did this? After they left my apartment, I felt like a knife had pierced my heart. It is so strange how pain can hit a person in so many ways. I honestly believed that if anyone should have known that it was not me doing this terrible thing that I was accused of, it should have been them. I did not know what to think. It sure did not build my self-esteem, and I did not feel worthy of asking God what was going on. I felt like crawling into the deepest part of the darkness that I was headed toward and getting lost from the reality that surrounded me. There are two important things that I have learned once you get closer to God. First, you learn about his love for you; and secondly, when you leave God's presence, the true identity of the devil is in full force.

The harassing situation with the members of the church continued. Until this day, I still do not know who was responsible, and I do not care. I do know that I still care for that family, and my love for them has never changed. I remember weeks before this incident surfaced, I went over to their house because they lost a loved one to an illness. Whatever I could do, I was willing to do. I remember buying a pair of shoes for one of the younger children to wear to the funeral. My heart was hurting for their loss, and God knew that I would not have done anything to bring more pain into their lives. The devil was busy, and I was his target. Several days had passed, and I felt like I did not know which way to go. The devil was having a field day in my mind and the surrounding area of my life. He was painting a perfect picture in my mind of what I thought people in the church were thinking of me. I now know that was his goal—to make sure that I wouldn't go back to the church. It was a place that once brought me comfort and gratitude. He knew that it was the only place for hope and survival. The devil knew what mattered to me, and if I felt the members of the church thought the worst of me, then I would not go back. Did they really think that I would do something that bad to someone I cared about? So many questions went through my mind. Didn't they know that I care about them, or did they ask God if I did what I was accused of doing? It didn't really matter if they did or not. The point was it was out there, and the people who heard about it could not do anything but wonder if it was true or not. I knew that God knew the truth, but it did not bring much comfort…because too many people were being victimized by the devil.

It was around the holidays, and it seemed like things were moving a little fast. As the days went by, I really did not know what I was going to do. I remember going to my parent's house to see my aunts who were visiting for the holidays. When I arrived at my parent's house, I walked into the living room. My mother had a letter in her hand, and she read it to me. My mom said that the member who thought I was harassing her family dropped the letter off to her earlier that day. Someone had written the letter and signed my name. My mother handed me the letter, and she told me that after she read the letter, she told the member that it was not my handwriting. My mother told me that she also told her that she did not believe that I was doing this horrible thing. That night, God gave me comfort, and the love my mother displayed that night gave me strength. It seemed like it did not matter anymore what people said or thought. The woman who gave me birth knew her child and that I would not do anything like that. That was all that mattered.

It is sad when you make a wrong turn in life and you have a label to follow. It is easy to assume the worst about a person when a person is not living his or her best, nor fulfilling the expectations of others. All that had happened was a hard pill to swallow. To think that the people who you were once close to would think the worst of you. I knew this family was hurting because of the recent death that had occurred in their family. Why did this family become convinced that it was me who wanted to hurt them and bring more pain to their lives? Perhaps it was because I was a backslider, and nothing else mattered. My feet felt like I was standing on a merry-go-round, and things were getting out of control. I needed a break from this cycle of darkness that was surrounding me.

Once again, I found myself sitting in my apartment, but this time a thick darkness was present. I was sitting on the floor with my back up against the wall. The depression was growing stronger every second. Then the clear words ran through my mind: "Get a knife from the kitchen." I found myself going to my kitchen and getting a knife. I sat back down on the floor in my living room with tears running down my face. Then I heard the same voice say, "Cut your wrist, and get it over with." I began to cry harder because I did not feel worthy of asking God for help. I looked at my risk, and I was about to cut it, and then a voice totally different from the first voice said, "If you die, you will end up in hell." Well, that wasn't a pleasant thought, because God had revealed too much in his word that he had to offer me that was so much better than hell. I knew enough that I didn't want to really end up there. So I dropped the knife, and I sat there and cried for hours. I finally got myself together enough to ask for help from God and to think rationally. The strength from my family was what I needed, and it was what God gave me to lean on.

I knew when my family stood up for me and their support was what I needed at this time.

Accusations will be made, and people will wonder if they are true—people who are in or out of the church. Sometimes, telling people you did not do something will not satisfy the doubt in their minds. I sometimes wonder if they sought God for the truth and asked him to reveal the person who was behind it all. One thing I knew for sure that night is I decided not to return to the church and be a part of anyone who was a part of it. We can assume whatever we want about one another, but the truth can only be revealed by God. This is especially for us who have confessed Jesus Christ and say we have a relationship with his Father and are led by his Holy Spirit. I have learned to trust in God and not what I see or think about people from my natural eyesight or understanding. With this experience in my life, I have learned to pray and seek God and to be lead by God's Holy Spirit in all that I do. God's sheep are precious to him regardless of the expectations we may place on one another. We must strive to handle one another with the love of God and by his Holy Spirit.

There were more negative things than positive things occurring in my life. The devil was truly busy, and he was on a roll. Being out of the ark of safety, my pride was hurting me, and shame was not far from me. I am not a cruel person, nor do I intentionally go out to hurt people. Yet at that time in my life, I felt like things seemed hopeless, and I was the one dying. As time passed, I knew I blamed the devil because I knew he was the one behind it all. However, I know he is not allowed to do any more than what God allows him to do. For us who are in Christ Jesus who have been given authority through the name of Jesus, we have authority in the name of Jesus over *all* the devils and their power.

When you are out of the ark of safety, the devil is going to do just what he is known to do to kill, steal, and destroy as many lives of those he can. The trick is that he was using me to assist him in something that he cannot do alone. I supplied the space in my mind for him to store the lies that gave him a way to set up a block from hearing the voice of my Lord calling me back to him. Understanding and knowledge from God are vital. The Holy Spirit brings revelation about God's holy word. I also believed that God allowed me to go the way he did, and he allowed me to go on this scenic route to see something that only he prepared for my eyes. This would grow and mature me to be the person that he wanted me to become. To this day, I love my first spiritual family who helped me to know about my Heavenly Father, his Son my Lord Jesus Christ, and the Holy Ghost. When I decided to leave Lufkin and moved to Houston, my thoughts were that I didn't want to be an embarrassment to God or the church. I went to a new place where no one knew me or about my past with the church. I soon learned that you will always make bad choices without the directions of God in your life.

MOVING ON

A Lost Sheep

There are many things we must endure with the church in order to grow as mature Christians. Over the years, I have heard several Christians say, "There's no hurt like church hurt." Now because my maturity in God has grown a little more, I suppose that Jesus could have said the same thing when he was crucified on the Cross or when he is denied daily.

You may be shunned by people, not get the recognition you deserve, talked about, or looked over. This may not allow you to go forward in God while you are in the church. Perhaps you gather with people who are more in tune with themselves than with God. Jesus endured so much with people who supposedly have known God. We learned in the word of God that they did not really know him or had a true relationship with him. Their actions spoke louder than their words, and they crucified our Lord. But do we crucify him afresh when we do not obey his word? I have learned living a Christian life is a growing process that can make you or break you. You are going to have to remain in the hand of God to endure all types of hurt, especially from those who assume to be Christ's representatives. I learned that you must view them through eyes as God's sheep and not human eyes. Viewing people through human eyes can cause you not to see them in the way that God intends for you to see them. Little did I know this with the first incident that I encountered or the next one to follow. However, I got there with the help of the Holy

Spirit, who has grounded me in a spiritual place with God that no one or nothing can take away from me.

It is such a blessing to look back on when I found myself as a backslider. It was difficult for me to face God and myself. It was years later that I knew that during my exit from him, he was still holding and keeping me from danger until it was time for me to hear him calling me back to him.

Yes, the devil had his field day, and he probably thought that he won the Superbowl with my soul. I did not know how much my heavenly Father loved me and how he allowed the hands of Satan just to go so far against me. To be honest, I thought that Satan had me, and I was about to let go. But God would continue to deal with me in dreams, and he would never let me go. Then one day, I heard these words? "God is married to the backslider." These words brought hope to a falling soul and again a little peace to my mind. I felt he was married to me and he would never let me go. I was the one who let him go, yet he would never let me go.

Unfortunately, I had not returned to church, and I continued to live my life in a world without God's direction. I ended up in a marriage to a young man who spoke smooth words and knew how to make a girl who was vulnerable and needed attention feel like she was the ideal choice for his life. I believed I was the one he needed to make his life complete. So I yielded to this smooth operator who spoke words that sounded like they would allow me some happiness in my life. I felt that I had endured enough pain for a while. I was old enough and believed I knew what I was doing. Although I was living a life without God, I was going to have the right relationship with this man as his wife and not as his woman who would live as a fornicator. We were married, and we made plans to move out of the state of Texas and start our new lives together as husband and wife. I gave my employer my two-week notice thinking something good was finally about to happen in my life. I went to my mother to tell her that I was going to get married, and she begged me not to. She said that it was not good and said not to do it. I did not listen and decided to marry, anyway.

I was married in December of 1983 and ready to start my new beginning with my new husband. We made plans to move to Louisiana, and since he was familiar with the location, he would travel there to set up the arrangements for us. He made two trips back and forth to Louisiana, leading me to believe that he was almost finished so that we could make our final move and live there. I was not stupid; I trusted my new husband and believed he was getting things together for us to make our move and live as husband and wife.

When he was away, I moved in with his mom. My mother-in-law was an extremely sweet person, and I stayed there, waiting for my new husband to return to get me. Time went by, and I had not heard from him in weeks. Then one day, I got a call from him, and he said that he was having problems and, as soon as he took care of this problem, he would come and pick me up to move to Louisiana. Days turned into weeks, and weeks turned into months, and eventually, he was nowhere to be seen. I was stuck in a place of dismay.

As days continued to pass, I found myself faced with a lie from a man who told me that he was going to take care of me and make everything all right. However, when reality kicked in, I realized the man I had married was not the prince charming, just an impersonator who knew how to play words to a wanting ear of loneliness. This brought hurt and shame in my life once again, and that weighed upon me heavily each day. Then the thoughts of feeling stupid began to pour into my mind. I quit my job and moved out of my apartment because this man told me that we were moving to a new location. Instead, I ended up living with his mother, and he was somewhere in the state of Louisiana, doing only God knows what. How much worse could things get? I found out that he was living with another woman and riding around in my car while I was living with his mother, waiting for him to return. This was my reality made for a TV movie without the director saying, "Cut."

I thought, "What more could happen in my life Lord?" One thing for sure is I knew I did not want to see my mother any time soon. I knew she was going to say what was on her mind. I had to face her. I went over to my parents' house, and my mama was sitting in the living room. I really did not say much, and I looked at her, and she said to me, "I told you." I could not get mad at what she said; she was telling the truth. She practically pleaded with me not to marry him. I just would not listen to her; now I wish I had. Yet this was just another lesson I had to learn the hard way.

I asked myself, "What did I get out of this marriage that would enable me to help someone not to make the same mistake I did?" Unfortunately, I could not find one thing at that time to help anyone, because I needed help in the darkness that I was in. I continued to stay with his mother. She was a loving woman. She was kind to me and always made me feel like her daughter. I had not seen my new husband for nearly four months after we were married, and my patience had worn very thin.

One Saturday night, my two brothers-in-law and I decided to ride around—to get out of the house. In the small town where we lived, it seemed like that was all you could do sometimes on a Saturday night. I was sitting in the backseat, just numb to everything that was happening in my life. I did not recognize the car that pulled up on the driver's side and slowly moved in front of the van that we were in. One of my brothers-in-law, who was driving, said, "Is that R?" The other brother-in-law, who was sitting in the passenger seat, said, "Yes." I leaned toward the front to see the car as it pulled in front of us. The car stopped long enough for me to read the license plate number. Something rose inside of me, and I looked at the familiar car that looked like my car. I looked at the license plate number on the car, which confirmed that it was my car. I immediately yelled out, "That's my car!" One of his brothers said, "That is not your car." I guess he was trying to calm me down. I knew that it was my car, and I told him that I knew that it was my car. We were going back and forth with one another, and this could have gone on forever between us, but I knew my license plate number, and nothing he said mattered. I insisted that they follow my car, and the brother driving refused to do so. I was getting angrier and angrier as my car pulled out of our sight. I wanted to get out and find someone to help me follow my car. I was hysterical! His brother refused to follow him, and as I watched him pull off, something inside of me changed for the worse. I continually asked his brother to follow him, and he refused. Then he began driving and was going slightly fast. I just wanted to get out. Nothing made sense. Even opening the door and jumping out of the van just to get to someone to help me seemed like a reasonable thing to do at the time.

Then my mind began to think of a way to make them think I was calm. I had to make them believe that I was rational and not act like a wife on *Snapped*. I suggested we go to this certain place just to see if that was my car or not. So they decided to go only if I would not attempt to get out of the van. I looked at them calmly and said, "I promise I won't try to get out." The anxiety grew more and more as we got closer. Everything but the child of God was raging up within me.

As we got to our destination and pulled up, I noticed my car parked in front of this club. My brother-in-law parked the van on the opposite side of the street, and the other brother came in the backseat to hold me so I would not try to get out. But before he could get back there, I was outside the van. I do not know how I got out so fast. I just knew that I was outside of the van standing face-to-face with the man who was called my husband. He looked at me with a smile on his face, and the next thing I knew is he slapped me. He told me that he did not want me to clown him. At that point, I felt like I was experiencing an out-of-body experience. I looked at him calmly with a slight smile on my face, and I thought, *You have not seen any clowning yet*. He told me to stay put while he talked with his brothers. I stood there in a semidaze, thinking that he just slapped me but all along pretending like I was going to be the good little wife as he instructed me to be. As he continued to talk with his brother, I eased one foot in front of the other and headed toward my car. As I got closer, I heard the voice of laughter. Wow, I heard people say everything seems like it is in slow motion when they face an event that can be ground shaking. I remember getting to my car and opening the front door on the passenger side. I saw a woman sitting in the front seat and a man with another woman sitting in the backseat. I never felt rage like that in my life. I knew she was the target, and she was in my car, and she had to go. When I opened the door, I heard her say,

"Hi." My eyes locked on her, and the emotions inside of me went out of control. All I wanted was for all of them to get out of my car. The next thing I remember was reaching for the woman and pulling her out of the front seat and beating her. All I felt was rage and anger. I snapped. My mind was not mine. I wanted them all out of my car. Then I was going for them in the backseat. I honestly believed if I had a gun that night, they would have been dead. The rage I felt was dark, something I never felt before. One of my brothers-in-law, whom I was close to. pulled me from the woman. My husband came to her defense, and he got back into the car and drove off. That was the last time I saw my car. I could not believe that he came to her defense and not mine. How could I trust him and feel that he cared for me? No, I was not naïve. I was just a sheep who had strayed too far from the light of God, wandering in unfamiliar darkness.

That night, I ended up at my parents' house. I went inside and sat on the couch and cried myself to sleep. I felt like I was near the edge of insanity. The next day, I just sat there all morning in the same spot, wearing the same clothes, and not saying anything. My mama would come into the room and look at me as though she did not know what to say, but she wanted me to know that she was there. Then my dad walked through the room, and he asked me to come and go with him. I slowly got up without saying a word and got into the car with him, and we drove off. He did not say anything. We just drove to different places to take care of some of his personal things. We finally made it back home, and we pulled into the driveway and sat in the car for a while. My dad said to me, "Pam, I only got one thing to say. We all make mistakes, but the best thing about making a mistake is we learn from it." I just broke down and started to cry. He looked at me and rubbed his hand on my head and said to me, "You will be all right." He got out and went into the house.

As I sat in the car crying, thoughts raced through my mind. I thought about the time when I told my mom that I was going to marry this man. I could only wonder if the Lord was dealing with my mom because she begged me not to do it. If I had listened to her, this part of my life would not have happened. After that happened, I found myself saying repeatedly, "Lord, I wished I listened to my mama." Now today I say, "Lord, thank you for taking me through the darkness and bringing me back into your marvelous light."

Days passed by, and there was no sign of R or my car. Looking over all things that had happened to me that year, I felt like my life was over. Unhappy and depressed, I needed a change. When was the change coming? I had no idea. My aunt who lived in Houston was visiting during this time, and she asked me if I wanted to move and go back to Houston with her. I told her yes, and she encouraged me more by saying I could get a job and live with her until I get back on my feet. I thought it wouldn't hurt, and I felt I needed a fresh start. Therefore, I left Lufkin and headed to Houston with my clothes, a little money, a broken marriage, and a heart filled with pain and shame. Sadly, I did not know how to handle it at all.

A JOURNEY BACK

Finding My Way Home

I moved to Houston in 1984. I was living with my aunt. I met Friend D; we became best friends. She was like a big sister to me. She would look after me and would not let anyone get over on me. She had street smarts and knew how to maneuver her way through things. I found myself hanging out with her, and we would have our good times together. Every chance I got to drown my sorrows by drinking or getting high, I would. Each day, this type of lifestyle became a pattern to find comfort. I thought it would take away the pain and shame, but it only drew me deeper into a darker hole of depression. Friend D and I were always together, and every time we could get high to bring laughter in our midst, we did it. I needed laughter in my life, even if it did not last a long time, to drown out everything else. She was a genuine friend who had a good heart. However, the times of trying to drown my pain were only temporary. My mind was not at peace, because I was running from the voice of God and the trouble of my past. The words from the Bible that had been taught and read were planted in my soul. My soul and mind were not connected at this time of my life. I tried to make sure to keep it separated. I was trying to cover the best thing that had been embedded within me, which was God's word from the worst things possible. I did this by going to the nightclubs and drinking to cover the pain. The funny thing is when Friend D and I would get high, I would witness to her about the Lord. She would sit there and listen and not say a word.

The next day, when we saw each other, she said if I would do it again, she would leave because I was scaring her and she would get sober.

I realized when we choose to live with our demons, the truth can be scary, especially when there is no true stability in our lives. It will become a fearful place to be because truth shows you where you are at that present time. God is all-powerful. He knows how to send a buzzkill. The status of my spiritual life for the next two years was inactive. Living with my aunt for a while, I got a job and eventually got my own apartment.

My attitude about men was extremely low. I decided that a man would never get the upper hand over me again. I was going to be the one in control and not them. So I dated just to get out of the house and have something to do. God knew I was not looking for love or to fall in love with anyone.

After being in Houston for a year, I dated and met another man, and he seemed to be different. I told him about my past and all about my baggage as time went by. But I did not think of anything, because I was not looking to get married anytime soon. After all, I was not divorced from the one who left me high and dry. Things in my life were complicated and incomplete, no matter how much I tried to do the club scene, have drinks with friends, or try to get away from my past. The day came when I realized that one cannot get away from one's past until they correct it. I knew that day would come. I just did not know when. I knew that I would have to go back and face the unfinished business that I was carrying into my present and hindering my future.

I realized I missed the relationship with my Heavenly Father, my Lord Jesus, and the Holy Spirit that I knew. They were the only ones who brought true happiness and peace into my life. Finally, that day came. It had been over three years since I left Lufkin, and the Lord was truly stirring my mind. There was no escaping him. When I was awake, thoughts of the Lord were heavy on my mind. I would dream, and I found myself wrestling in my sleep. There was no peace. Nothing could ease it, and each day got worse. There was a pressing feeling that I needed to go home and visit my family. So I went home one weekend, but my decision was more than just spending time with my family. The Lord was stirring my mind to go to visit my home church. This feeling was different, and I could not shake it. I tried to ignore it. I knew it would be detrimental on my end. I did not want to go, but this overwhelming feeling of urgency was pressing upon me to go to church.

I made it to my parents' house that Saturday morning. I spent time with my mom and stayed around the house for a little while. Then I had a visit from an old friend. It was Friend B. I had not seen her in years. We decided to drive to the zoo and sit in the park and talk for a while. Our conversation was pleasant, but we did not have much to say. I remember her asking me about the family who accused me of harassing them. She wanted to know if I did it. Before I could answer her, she said that she did not believe that I could do that.

My immediate thought was if that were so, then why would she ask that now? But I just stared at her with a slight smile on my face, feeling disappointed. I gave her the same truthful answer as always: "No." I did not know if she was convinced or not, but it really didn't matter. Later that evening, I went back to my parents' house and stayed for a while with my mama until night. I decided that I would go out that night. I went out to the club, and once I got there, it was not the same. I felt very uncomfortable sitting in that place. The club scene was dull, and I eventually went home.

I got up Sunday. It was May 1986. That morning, I got up, and I felt a hesitation to go to church. Old thoughts began to flood my mind of what people would say. However, there was a stronger feeling that was drawing me to go, and I knew if I did not go, this would be my last chance. Without further hesitation, I knew that I had to go to church and decided to go. When I walked into the sanctuary, I was so nervous and very ashamed. Everything wrong about me seemed to be noticeable, and it seemed like the eyes of people were glued on me, but I did not give much eye contact. I moved further into this new building to find a seat in the far back. The service began, and the choir sang with the anointing of God's Spirit, and God's presence was there. At last, I was in a safe place with the presence of God.

As the pastor began to preach, the anointing of God's word found the damaged place in my heart where I felt worthless. I knew I belonged to him. The preached word rested on my heart, and his Spirit covered me like a warm blanket on a winter night. I had not felt that free in an awfully long time. I really did not know what to expect that day. Every thought imaginable was passing through my mind—thoughts of leaving my life in Houston or whether I should move back to Lufkin. However, the only things I should have focused on were connecting with God and getting my life back in order.

The Spirit of God continued to move in that place, and people were crying out to the Lord. Then the Spirit of God overshadowed me, and all I could say was, "Yes, Lord." I began to tell my heavenly Father that I was sorry, and I asked him to forgive me. I told him that I would give up everything to be back in his presence and surrender all to get back to him. His Spirit began to cover me like arms holding a newborn baby, and tears were rolling down my face.

The pastor's wife came to me in the back, and she led me to the altar. I began to cry more, "Yes, Lord, yes to your will!" The next thing I knew was that I was speaking in tongues, and the Lord reclaimed his backslider, what was rightfully his. I was filled with the precious Holy Spirit. I was delivered and set free. Hallelujah! I was embraced by my brothers and sisters in the Lord who were welcoming me back.

Nothing else mattered. It was a new start, a new beginning. My past was over. I felt that the devil no longer could walk in my presence or hinder the plans God had for my future. I did not dwell on anything from my past. All I knew was that my heavenly Father had placed me back into his fold, and nothing else mattered. I was no longer a lost sheep trying to make it home. I was home—home in his presence and covered with his *love*! I was God's sheep; and my eyes clear on his view of love, peace, and happiness for my life. I was ready to be led on the path that he had for me, to fulfill his purpose for my life. After church, I made it back to my parents' house, and my mom was in the kitchen cooking Sunday's dinner. I sat at the bar, and I was not saying much. I told her that the Lord reclaimed my soul, and I was filled with the Holy Ghost that day. She smiled and continued to cook dinner. There was a long silence. Then she said something I least expected, but it was on my mind. She said, "If Anthony loves you, he will ask you to marry him." That brought a smile to my face, but I did not worry about that. At least she was not in tears like the first time I told her I wanted to get married. I was glad that my peace was restored, and the joy of the Lord was back in my life. I left Lufkin that day to head back to Houston. I believe that God would direct my path from that day forward.

I made it back to Houston late that evening. I called Anthony and told him that I needed to talk with him. We agreed to meet the next day. We met, and I shared with him my experiences that had occurred over the weekend. I told him that I could no longer live the lifestyle that I once was living, nor could our relationship be the same as before. He looked at me with a slight smile on his face, and we agreed that we would remain friends but live our lives pleasing unto God.

We continued to go out on dates and do things together. He truly respected my decision, but I really admired him because he respected God's decision for my life. We believed that if anything good was going to happen in our lives as a couple, we had to do what was right before God. There was still one thing I needed to do, and that was to contact my first husband and take care of business between him and me. I had not seen him in over two years and did not know how to contact or reach him. So I got a lawyer to start the divorce process.

He was located, and I explained to him that all I wanted from him was for him to sign the divorce papers. Well, I thanked God he signed, and my lawyer filed the paper. The only thing I wanted to give him back was his name. I did not want to carry it any longer, because it brought pain and hurt to my life.

It was June 1986. Anthony and I were at his house in the living room, and he was recording gospel music on a cassette tape for me. Our relationship was platonic. We were good friends. I had accepted the possibility that we might end up going our separate ways and I probably would be moving back to Lufkin. That night, I sat quietly on the couch as Anthony recorded the music on the cassette tape.

THROUGH THE EYES OF A SHEEP

He began to write something on a piece of paper. I thought they were the songs he was recording for me on the cassette tape. He turned around, and he handed me the folded piece of paper. I slowly took the piece of paper from his hand and opened it and read the words "Will you marry me?" I took the pencil and wrote, "Yes," on the same piece of paper, folded it, and gave it back to him. He looked at it, put it in his pocket, and continued to finish recording the music. Three months later, we were married—on October 25, 1986; and we have been together for thirty-eight years and counting.

BECOMING ONE

Placed and Position by God

God blessed Anthony and me to share our lives together, and begin a beautiful family. The following year, we had our firstborn, a son, whom we named Tony. We were happy and content, the three of us. We had committed to live our lives to please God. Our priority was to find a church and go as a family. We attended a church here in Houston that was affiliated with my home church in Lufkin. We were excited about going, and Anthony was serious about giving his life to the Lord and seeking the Holy Spirit. It was a small church that reminded me of the church at home with a few members. I thought it was great because it would give us an opportunity to grow together and become a strong spiritual family in God. We were determined whatever God wanted us to do, we would do our best to accomplish it. I was happy, and I felt that we were on the right road and the only thing we had to face was the devil and his works. Not really focusing on the devil doing all he could to stop the progress of God for our lives, we were happy to be a family and going to church and pleasing God.

  The excitement grew, and anything we could find our hands to do in serving God and those around us, we were willing to do so. We would have church outings after Sunday services and go eat with the members. We had about twenty members total at the time. The one thing we wanted was God to add to the church. The brethren would work around the outside of the church, and the sisters would work on the inside. Everyone got to know everyone, and it seemed like the love was growing stronger. Nearly three years had passed, and everything seemed to be going well. Every year, we would have an anniversary service for the pastor and his wife. The church from Lufkin would come and be a part of the fellowship in showing appreciation in encouraging our new pastor and his wife.

I noticed that every time after this service, the pastor would come back the following week and preach about love. I really did not think anything of it. I just sat there and listened to his message. I noticed that it became the same topic each year during the same event every year. The pastor would come forth and give his same remark about love.

One day, while attending church on a Sunday morning, the pastor asked the congregation to come up for prayer. We were such a small group. It was about a total of fifteen people all together. The Pastor would go around and lay his hands on each person and pray for them. When he came to me, he placed his hand on my forehead and began to pray. I noticed that he was pressing his fingers in the temple on the side of my head, and he began to say, "I bind Satan. I bind Satan." I thought, *was he talking about me being Satan?* He was there for a while, and then he released his hand and went to someone else.

After church, on our way home, I discussed it with Anthony. We did not know what to think, and we just pushed it off and continued to go to church as usual. I became a little uneasy, and all I wanted to do was to keep my husband encouraged in the Lord. My husband was new in the church, to holiness and the Holy Ghost. I knew a bit more than he did. I knew I had much to learn, but one thing I did know for sure was that the devil was not in me. Yes, he tried to destroy me before, and he did his job well. Fortunately, this time, I was not helping him with this task. This was my spiritual leader, and his attempt in trying to bind Satan in me was unacceptable.

As days went by, we continued to attend church and fellowship with everyone. Then it was time for another anniversary service. The same thing happened again with the pastor preaching about love at the next church service. His message became redundant. I thought,

Where was he trying to go with this message? This anniversary service was a good one. Everyone was happy, and it seemed like we were all headed toward higher ground in the Lord. The following week, we planned to attend our weekly service. Anthony and I went to church that night thinking that we would hear good feedback about the previous services. The pastor began making indirect comments about us not showing love toward one another. By this time, it was becoming very annoying, and I felt like he should get over it already. He attempted to bind the devil in me that was not there. He spoke about not showing love toward members in the church during this certain event every year.

Then the unexpected happened. The pastor called for a meeting for the few members who were attending. If I had known that I would be the center of attention that night, I probably would have stayed home. The comments about not showing love were being directed at me. I was the target of his sermon about love, saying that I wasn't showing love. The pastor stood before everyone who were present and commented that someone was showing partial love toward someone else. He then turned the floor over to his sister-in-law, who presented her complaint toward me. She stood up and said that I ignored her and treated her unkindly when our guest church was visiting during the pastor and his wife's anniversary service. After she made the comment toward me, the pastor said, "Uh oh!" I could not believe my ears. It was like we were on the street and someone was trying to stir up a fight.

Then he said that every time the people from Lufkin would come to visit, I would show love toward them more than I would toward the members there. I just sat there in awe, thinking Lord, *What is going on?* Immediately, I felt the same way from the incident in Lufkin. I thought, *Oh no, is this happening again?* I was being accused of something that I did not do. I was utterly lost for words. When I stood up to speak, I looked at the pastor's sister-in-law and asked her if she felt that I had mistreated her in any way. I asked her why didn't she come to me, but she did not give me an answer that made sense to me. It was like déjà vu. That spirit I felt when I was in Lufkin during the time I was accused of harassing that family was there again. But I did not know how to handle it. I did not know about spiritual warfare. Whom could I tell, and who would believe me? I know now this dark presence was following me, and he had an assignment, and I must say he was doing a surprisingly good job. Dark spirits like this only need weak vessels or vessels that lack the knowledge and wisdom of God to operate.

During that time, I was in no position to battle, and no one was there to help me fight. I did the only thing that I was led to do—sit there and listen to the accusations of my accusers. I was listening to the pastor talk about me not showing love that he had preached so many times before to his small congregation. When they were finished with their comments, the only thing the Holy Ghost allowed me to say was, "If I have been a hindrance to anyone in this church, I ask you to forgive me. But I will not be back to this church unless God tells me to come back." Afterward, I got my Bible and politely went and, sat in the car, and waited for my husband and cried. I was told later by another member that my husband expressed his opinion about how I was targeted that night. She said he asked them why it was so hard for them to understand my relationship with my former spiritual leaders whom I have known since the beginning of my walk with the Lord. Love is the thing that should bring us together in church. But at that time, it was what they used to drive us out. We both left that night and did not return.

For the next fourteen years, my husband did not attend church. He would look at his television ministry faithfully every Sunday morning. I went to church with the children while faithfully hoping and praying that one day he would join us. The years went by, and it would be a long time before we sat together as a family inside of a building and worshipped God together. I did not give up, and I continued in prayer to God, waiting for a change to take place in our lives for him and our family. This time, the devil did not have me on the run. I had to learn how to stand and face him the way God intended for me. Not knowing fully how that would be, I had to trust God and believe that he had me. The devil tried to wreak havoc in our marriage and our lives over the years. The more he stirred, the more I prayed unto God, and the more he would strengthen me to endure. I was not the same person Satan wanted me to believe I was, who left running confused and hurt. This time, I knew to run unto the Lord. Proverb 18:10 (KJV) says, "The name of the LORD is a strong tower: the righteous runneth into it and is safe." I was a little bit mature in Christ and was more aware of the enemy's tricks. I knew that I was not perfect, but I knew who to turn to, and that was my Lord and Savior Jesus Christ. He helped me reach perfection in the areas where I needed help. The Holy Ghost gave me strength and guided me on the path God intended for my life. I knew that the devil was trying to kill two birds with one stone. I just refused to let him make me and my family become his targeted birds. I had enough in me to seek God continually for strength and wisdom every chance I got. The Lord taught me how to humble myself in him. If I could not humble myself in him, I sure could not humble myself before others. I found myself praying, "Lord, place me in your will. Make me to be who you want me to be." There were many nights that I would shed tears, but the tears made me strong. I was in a place that only God knew. I believed that every time a tear fell, he would catch it. Although, the situation did not change right away, and there were times when I would have to bear confusion in my household caused by the devil. The more he showed up, the more I recognized him, and the more determined I became to stand my ground. He did not care about me, and I did not care about him. I did not realize how afraid the devil was of me, because God had instilled in me his Holy Spirit and power. I had grasped onto an attitude that remains the same today; there is nothing that I cannot handle without God. He does not need me, but I need him. I was willing to be used in any way that he wanted. He will not put any more on me than I could bear. This is one of the key elements to my success in God, and I learned it the hard way. First Corinthians 10:13 (KJV) says, "There hath no temptation taken you but such as is common to man: but God is faithful, who will not suffer you to be tempted about that ye are able; but will with temptation also make a way to escape, that ye may be able to bear it."

Therefore, I did what I had to do to stay close to my God. I would travel every other weekend to Lufkin and visit my home church until I found another church to attend in Houston. All I wanted was to find a good church home with a strong shepherd—one who would lead me and my family according to the will and word of God. My husband was faithful to his television ministry every Sunday morning. The only time we went together after the incident was when the TV pastor would visit from Los Angeles and was scheduled to come to Houston. There were times I wanted to write to this pastor and ask him to let my husband know he needed to do better and go to church with his family and if he could please announce it on television. I know really…but sometimes thinking about some things will give you a little ease.

I was never alone. My Heavenly Father, my Lord and Savior Jesus Christ, and the Holy Ghost were there for me through thick and thin; and I thanked God for that. Therefore, I learned to place everything in God's hands on the knowledge that he had given me at the time, because he knew how to work out any situation in the lives of his sheep.

I knew a change was taking place within me spiritually, but I could not understand the process of what God was doing to me. He was molding me for the tasks that he had designed for my life. Oh, it is not easy, and I am far from being who God intends for me to be completely. One thing I do know is when I am in his presence, the excitement of being there motivates me to continue to go farther. I would find myself fasting and praying more. I learned the more I sought his will, the more he drew to me, and the more I had to face life's trials; however, it didn't matter, because I was closer to him. James 4:8 (KJV) says, "Draw nigh to God, and he will draw nigh to you. Cleanse your hands, ye sinners; and purify your hearts, ye double minded."

SHAKING BUT UNMOVABLE

Time to Move Forward in God

It was December 31, 2004, and I was at church that evening, getting ready to bring in the New Year with the Lord. Again, I found myself praying to God for his help and guidance for me and my family. We had come to the point where we needed the Lord to help and guide us in the direction that he needed us to go. When the children and I left Lufkin that evening, all I could do was hold on to God and trust him that he will make everything all right between Anthony and me. He would help us to walk together once again as man and wife worshipping him in the same sanctuary. Driving that night from Lufkin, it seemed like the closer I got home, the tension grew heavier. When I made it home, unloaded the car, and put the children in bed, I went into my bedroom. I believed that at this point, Anthony was going to do whatever he wanted. As I entered the bedroom, I was completely lost for words. I prayed to God, and I said to him, "Father, I don't know what to say. Please lead me and give me what to say to him." I sat on the side of the bed, and I took a breath. I looked at him and said we needed to talk. As usual, he lay there and did not say much. I took a deeper breath, and I continued to pray before I said another word. God knew I did not want to mess it up. I said to him, "If we are going to go anywhere in God, we must be one in this marriage in every way." I told him that we needed God and it was time for us to decide to put God first in our lives again as a couple. He said,

"Okay." I thought, *Oh my God!* Hearing the word *okay* coming from his mouth was music to my ears. I was happy, and I began to thank God for what he was doing. I believed that everything was going to be all right for us. This was the time for us to move forward in God, and now God had opened the door of opportunity for us to begin this journey together once again.

My next prayer was for God to help us make the right decision in attending a church where we could grow spiritually in him under a spiritual leader who will help bring us closer to him. When we made our decision on what church we would be attending, I called my former pastor and his wife in Lufkin to tell them what was taking place in our lives. After giving them the news of how God helped us in deciding which church to attend, they were happy for us. My former pastor said that he would make a call to the pastor of the new church and speak to him on our behalf. He called the pastor of the new church and informed him that my family and I would be attending and would be under watch-care. We began our new journey in the new church as a family—Anthony, our three children, and me.

A couple of years passed, and we were faithfully attending church as a family. I sought the Lord because I wanted to go higher in him spiritually. Then the Lord began to deal with me in certain ways. He would bring things to my attention that were disturbing. At first, I tried to push it off because I really did not want to mess up the family thing of going to church together. I was praying and asking God what was going on and hoping it was not me. I found myself fasting and praying and seeking God more. I wanted to be active in the church and wanted to win souls for Christ. However, that was not the case. The Lord was taking me on a path that would bring out something that would not be accepted by those whom I had to face. After a year in church, my husband was chosen to be a deacon. He was still seeking God and seeking for the Holy Ghost, but he was faithful, and he did whatever they would ask him to do in assisting in the church as much as possible. My husband is a good man, and when he commits himself to something, he is committed.

There was a shift in the church, and things began to change spiritually. I found myself asking God what was wrong and why I was feeling the way I was feeling. The Holy Ghost was leading me in a direction that only God could approve of and understand. He began to deal with me in dreams on the behavior of certain people in the church. I know the Bible informs us that the wheat and tare will grow together. Therefore, when Jesus comes back, he will perform the separation. But this was not about trying to separate anyone from the church; it was about acknowledging their wrong. I would ask God, "Why me?" These people were looked up to. I know when the Lord chooses someone, he will have them go before his people to say what he wants them to say whether it is good or bad. If that person is you, then you had better be ready to be obedient unto the Lord. As God continued to deal with me, I was feeling like, "Who was I to go and tell anybody anything?" So I tried to fix it by smiling and going with the flow of the things in the church, but it was not working. The more I tried to push it away, the more the Lord would stir my mind to do what he wanted me to do. One thing I have learned is when God speaks to you, you speak. He does not care how much you try to avoid the task; it is not going away until you complete what God wants you to do.

Nearly three years passed, and things in the church were not getting better. People were not stable, and they would come and go. There was this one Hispanic mother who joined with her two children. She came to service, and she would praise God and enjoyed fellowship with the members of the church. One Wednesday night during Bible study, an incident occurred in the sanctuary. The lights only in the sanctuary went off. I know that this does not sound unusual, but it was *how* the lights went out. There was no bad weather outside, and the lights were on in the other buildings and in the community. However, the lights went out three times; and on the third time, it was total darkness. As the people were getting up and scattering in the sanctuary, the Spirit of the Lord told me to watch. As I looked and saw the reaction of the people, they were walking in darkness, and this lady went to get a flashlight to give to the pastor to continue reading the word of God from his Bible in the darkness. Then the Spirit of the Lord spoke to me and said, "You cannot read my words in the darkness." As I sat there continuing to watch the action of the people, the Spirit of the Lord said to me, "My mouthpiece is dull, and until he gets it right with me and the church, I will not lift him." As those words continued to flow in my mind, the lights came back on in the church. Then the Spirit of the Lord laid it upon my heart to tell his mouthpiece the words that I heard the Spirit say. Then suddenly, the Hispanic mother rushed into the church, crying hysterically in outburst toward the pastor, saying, "God said you lie, you lie." All I could feel was distress and heaviness. That mother left that night with her children and never returned. The weight that I felt remained heavy on my heart, and nothing I did could lift it.

The words the Lord said to me that night would linger not only on my mind but also in my heart. The Lord directed me to tell these words to the pastor. I knew what the Spirit of God was directing me to do. I also knew that it would be downhill for me once those words came out of my mouth and into the ears of this pastor. I trusted God and loved him more than man, and my status in man is nothing unless God has placed me there. I knew that God was moving me forward in him, and even though some would not understand, I knew it wasn't for them. It was for the positioning of my life in God. The Lord let me know that you must be spiritual to understand spiritual things, and when you are dealing with people who are not spiritual, they will not understand the things of God.

So as days went by, I would carry the heaviness that the Lord had placed on me to tell the pastor. Time had gone by, and I had not done what the Lord had instructed me to do. Then one Sunday, as I was ushering, the Spirit of the Lord began to move in the sanctuary. It was time for people who wanted prayer to go to the altar. I stood back, and I watched the people go up. The Spirit of the Lord told me to go and speak the words that he told me that night to say to the pastor. I asked the Lord how I should go, and the Spirit instructed me to go through the prayer line. As I walked up and stood face-to-face to him, he leaned toward me, and I told him the words that the Lord said to me that night, and he leaned a second time, and I repeated the same words to him. He only looked at me and did not say a word. I turned and walked away. As I walked away, the heaviness that I had been carrying for weeks was lifted off me. It did not matter anymore if I was accepted by a man or a woman. The acceptance of God was what I needed to go forward on this journey.

    I knew that God had directed my husband and me there, and through obedience, we did as God led us at that present time. But it wasn't until years later that I came to understand his purpose in putting me in that position. One thing I've learned is that you can become a distraction when man places you, instead of allowing God to place you in the position for his purpose. Yes, I thought I would be accepted, but what was not accepted was what God had placed in me spiritually. I know it is not about me, but it is all about God. I truly do not want to be anywhere God is not accepted. I heard when God instructed me to go, and I heard him when he instructed me to leave. Individuals must obtain a relationship with God to hear from him in these present times. Sometimes we become satisfied in what God has instructed us to do ten, twenty, or thirty years ago, as though He stops speaking to us. Jesus said, "My sheep, hear my voice." and I believe he speaks to us on a daily basis so that we can move closer to God. What is God saying to you now? Do you have a relationship with him wherein you can hear him in this present time? I pray that I will always have an ear for God. Every day, I longed to be closer to him and communicate with him. I would acknowledge him daily, so he would direct my path in this present world. Proverbs 3:6 (KJV) says, "In all thy ways acknowledge him, and he shall direct thy path."

STANDING FOR GOD

Stay in the Race

I have learned that anything in this life is not worth having if it leads you from the kingdom of God. The blessings of God are priceless, and you will have to be willing to surrender yourself to ensure that you receive everything God has for you while you are here on earth. Our Lord and Savior Jesus Christ has paid the price so we can have what is priceless of God. The day I died in self and surrendered my life to God, everything that he offered me was more than I could ever imagine. Living with him daily in faith increases through my trials and circumstances, receiving his unconditional love, and having a mind filled with the peace of God. I refused to let the devil have any of it, even though he comes to steal, kill, and destroy; but every day, I learn about his ways and how he operates. People may not always be who they say they are. Attending church is not like attending a sports event where you gather to get your yell on. We attend church to praise and worship our heavenly Father with our brothers and sisters in Christ. In order to grow stronger and receive what God has for us, we must become better people and help one another and those in need.

I know on this final path; the devil is not going to give up, especially now since God has positioned me in the direction of completing my journey home with him. I know the devil will cause more havoc with family members, friends, coworkers, strangers, and especially those in the body of Christ. I know that my heavenly Father will continue to help me to trust in him, and I will continue to pray as the Spirit of God will lead me to pray. In that, I can be spiritual and face every situation the way God has me to face it. I know that God is in control of everything around me because I have learned to acknowledge him. Sometimes, when my physical strength is nearly gone, God continues to guide me by the Holy Ghost, who gives me strength, and I praise him for the comforter. Jesus said in John 14:16 (KJV), "And I will pray the Father, and he shall give you another Comforter, that he may abide with you forever."

For years, I was waiting for God for answers for my life's trials and situations. He is helping me to continue to wait for him for direction for the lives of my family and others. He has allowed each of us to make decisions to get closer to him. I pray that my family and loved ones make sound decisions in seeking him with their whole hearts, minds, and souls. There are times when things become unbearable and seem like everything is drifting further apart. These are the times when I have learned to hold to God's unchanging hand and not to give up. This is when he takes over and shows his strength and might in my life.

It is so easy to focus on people, even though watching their every move may bring pleasure and disappointments. When I was a child, I saw things without definition, just the beauty of God's creation. The more I walk with God, the more I see things through the definition of God's eyes. The beauty of God's love, peace, joy, and protection was always there for me, especially when I didn't know it existed. It is an assurance that someone is watching over me. I am a sheep in God's fold, and my vision sees through the faith that God has placed in my heart to hold on to him and his word and to love others as he loves me. The different views that we pick up from the negative opinions, the disappointments, and frustration during a lifetime can keep us from achieving and accepting what God truly has for his children. I made many mistakes in my life, but I can honestly say that I have learned from all of them. I strive not to repeat the same mistake. I know I will make new mistakes, but this time, I am not walking alone. I strive to have my five spiritual senses in tune with the Lord as the Holy Spirit leads me. With each situation far or near, I pray that I see it as God wants me to see; therefore, I can be a help and not a hindrance to those who are involved. I believe if you are truly a sheep in the fold of God and you pray and seek God's help, the sheep hears the voice of Jesus directing its path. The Holy Spirit is waiting to lead us to become sons and daughters of God. It will not be easy, and many obstacles will get in our way until we make it to heaven. I know that I can do all things through Christ, who strengthens me!

For many years, my husband and I were not balance, because of the lack of knowledge not provided from our earthly spiritual leaders on spiritual warfare to help and guide us in our spiritual walk in the Lord. Sometimes, it is meant for people to walk together, and then there are times when you must walk alone. Either way, I believe as an individual, it is our personal responsibility to seek God through prayer and studying his word. The Holy Spirit is doing and will continue to do his job, and that is to lead us to leaders who are chosen by God. We must stop seeing things as it is and begin to see as God sees it and pray that it becomes as he wants it to be.

My prayer to God is to bless every sheep in his fold and those who have strayed away, those who are blind and deaf to what the Spirit is saying in this present hour. The body of Christ needs spiritual shepherds who are connected to God and who are hearing from him daily, so the body of Christ can be one in unity all over the world by his Holy Spirit.

I would visit churches, but it was nothing like having your own spiritual leader so that you can have a covering over your soul. Therefore, I could not afford to sit under just anyone because he or she says they have been called by God. There must be a spiritual connection between God and the leader that draws us together. My heart and mind were seeking God for spiritual growth. I honestly believed that God had more for me to do, and it was about kingdom priorities of getting about my father's business. God has brought me to understand the things in my life that directed me to go the way he has chosen for me to go.

I am not the little girl who sees things through make-believe eyes, but I have a clear view now since Jesus has opened my eyes.

The view that I see is an encouraging view, and I am focused on a heavenly gain.

Living my life in Christ every day, each step brings me closer to Him, as the Holy Ghost leads me on my path. I know where I am headed, and I must remain focused on God. I thank God for the Holy Ghost because he refuses to encompass darkness. We are in a time where God is calling his true shepherds to get his sheep ready. When the true word of God is being preached in the churches and the people are totally seeking the righteousness of God, then the people of God will not be troubled about the things now or things to come. I don't go to church out of familiarity. I go because I need a real word from God, and I need the shepherd of the house to hear from God. My soul is hungry for the truth and righteousness of God. Over the years, my relationship with God and his word has become stronger, and the bond that kept me in tune with God is the Holy Ghost, and the foundation is his beloved Son, my Savior Jesus Christ.

We are living in an era where people believe you must obtain a certain status before they believe anything you have to say. Well, Jesus has the highest status, and even today some still do not believe. Therefore, I am on a mission. When God tells me to do something or say something, I am going to be obedient and allow the Holy Spirit to lead me. Those who have an ear to hear, let them hear what the Spirit of God has to say to his church. Those who are of God will know the things of God and will not reject it. If you are led by the Spirit of God, who dwells inside of you, it's time to go forth in the name of the Lord Jesus Christ. People will try to place you, but strive so God will position you for his kingdom.

I am stronger in the Lord, and I strive to walk by the Spirit of God. God has allowed me to be under pastors who are seeking the heart of God—spiritual shepherds who believe in the word of God and are filled with the Holy Ghost. There are many pastors and spiritual leaders all over the world who have compassion for the people and love to teach the words of Jesus Christ so the purpose of God will manifest on earth. Earthly shepherds must be spiritual and led by God's Spirit to know and care for the sheep. Jesus asked Peter in

John 21:15 three times if he loved him, and then Jesus replied feed my sheep.

I realized that this war is not against flesh and blood but the spiritual darkness of this world. Am I ready to move forward? Yes, because I am more than a conqueror. God has equipped me for this journey. But I know he has more for me in this lifetime. I need to be strong and under a Spirit-led shepherd who has been chosen by God in this world to guide me.

My Heavenly Father, whom I serve, owns everything; and I find him to be a rewarder to those who diligently seek him. Matthew 6:33 (KJV) says, "First seek ye the kingdom of God and all his righteousness and all the things will be added unto you." So I have learned to put God first. I thank him for my Lord and Savior Jesus Christ, the one who died for me and opened a door so I could know our Heavenly Father.

My attitude is that I am moving forward in God. Too much is happening in this world, and I cannot afford to sit under someone who is not hearing from God.

I pray that in reading these words, you are encouraged and seek God daily. Ask him for spiritual ears and eyes. Most importantly, pray to him that he will keep the leaders he has placed over the body of Christ to be Spirit led and spiritual minded in their walk with Christ and have the love of God, that they may continue to hear from him. If you find yourself in need of a spiritual shepherd, pray that God will lead you to a pastor after his own heart. A pastor after God's heart will stay in tune with God.

Life is full of many changes, changes that consist of good and evil. These changes will affect everyone until our Lord Jesus Christ returns to this world. This is something that I honestly believe will happen as the days draw near.

I heard many encouraging words spoken and written down through the years from believers who say that they know God and have a word for the people—words that would bring hope to help others hold on to their faith in God. I can honestly say that I am hopeful in God and his powerful words to finish the course he has prepared for my life according to his will. There are many things I have seen in my lifetime from different perspectives. There is always someone looking in from the outside, and there are those who are looking out from the inside. But I thank God for the eyes of a sheep that are directed from his viewpoint and not man's viewpoint. The hardest view for any child of God to focus on is without the help of a true spiritual shepherd of God filled with the Holy Ghost.

I believe that God has appointed many spiritual Holy Ghost–led leaders for his sheep all over the world who and are waiting for the appointed time that the Holy Spirit will lead us all as onefold to accomplish the kingdom work of God here on earth. Through the eyes of the sheep, we will see as God sees and move as he directs us by his Spirit.

This is when the work of darkness is bound in the body of Christ and the deliverance of God is manifested. Jesus said that "My sheep know my voice." True leaders get their instructions from God to help the sheep to develop strength that enables them to walk strong, to be knowledgeable and have wisdom, to speak the truth, and, most importantly, to have the vision to see the works of the enemy. This is when the sheep of God becomes not only a hearer of the word but also a doer of God's word.

When people sit under weak leaders, then the sheep become weak, and they scatter and lose ground. They cannot see because their vision is poor and their ears are dull. They will then just sit and watch for years, praying to God to bring them out of a spiritual drought. The leader loses spiritual insight from God and only sees before him a destitute gathering of people he cannot help, but he does not hear the directions of God. Therefore, the leader is yet drilling them to believe that everything is okay, and God will answer their call. We as people are so naïve to believe in anything that will bring comfort in our lives. What is true comfort? I believe that is when we obtain a true and real relationship with God as a father and child. I can say, "I no longer see through my eyes that have been contaminated by the views of those around me and who don't hear from God. They have failed to continue their walk with him. Those whose eyes have become dull and cannot see for personal gain. Therefore, I pray that I live my life as God's child who is led by his Spirit and not a child who can be led away easily due to despair.

I will live the rest of my life looking through the eyes as one of God's sheep with a spiritual viewpoint. I must stay in the true pasture (the presence of God) because it is almost time to go home. I see with compassion and love. I pray that God's will be done on earth as it is in heaven. Now is the time for every sheep of God in the body of Christ all over the world to focus and not have dull eyesight or itching ears. Jesus has promised us that he will give us abundant life. This is the truth of God's word and the outpouring of his Spirit.

We must pray for our leaders to remain true to God every day. The enemy's plan is to destroy every believer in the house of faith, especially when the vision of the leader is blurred and the sheep are scattered. Only God can give us true insight toward the step we must take in our lives, and the direction we are headed. I know what we see every day can cause us to lose hope for what God has prepared for his believers. I pray that these words will be a blessing to every reader in Jesus's name.

Yes, I was faced with many elements that guided me in directions that brought happiness and pain, but these elements became learning tools as I continued to walk the path with eyes wide open or partially closed. By God's grace, we may find our way back to him from the place that drew us further away from him. Thank God for the Spirit-led shepherds who are praying for the lost sheep and seeking those who have strayed away. A person often figures out the reasons things happen in his or her life when they have returned back to the fold of God. Then there are people who will never understand or care about why things happened the way they did in their lives. They choose to go with the everyday flow of existence and leave this world without ever knowing why they were born into this world. I thank my Lord and Savior Christ Jesus for allowing me the opportunity to express the intimacy, which I have captured from his love for me and the love of my heavenly Father and the Holy Spirit.

In this book, my goal is to touch someone and share with them my experiences. I pray the eyes that read these words will see the love, joy, hope, and closure that were brought to me through my relationship with my Heavenly Father, through his loving Son, my Savior Jesus Christ and the Holy Spirit. I also pray that this book will encourage and strengthen each reader to hold stronger to his or her faith in God. Things around us may not be what we think they should or look the way we think they ought to look, but if we hold to our faith in God in due season, we shall reap the goodness of God if we faint not.

I believe that we do not have to wait until we get to heaven to reap the goodness of God, because he wants us to reap it here on earth right now. What I used to see, I do not see anymore. My view has changed. It is now the view through the eyes of a sheep that is destined to walk the designed path chosen by God. I realized the things that I focused on in the early stage of my life displayed meanings that were far from the truth. Yet the imitation of them brought temporary excitement, joy, pain, and despair. I know now that every day God has blessed me to see the picture of my life vividly in him with a true understanding that comes from him. The expectations of men do not define me, but who I am in God defines every expectation of the life that he has designed for me.

I am his sheep, a part of his fold, and I was created in my mother's womb by his hands to walk the path set up by him. God's *amazing grace* is truly sweet. I was blind but now I see, and I thank God that he saved a wretch like me.

FINALLY, CLARITY

When you think of the five senses that were given to us, which one would you think is the most important one? I believe the average person would say all of them: sight, hearing, smell, taste, and touch. I would agree. However, I believe as we take the steps through our spiritual journey, seeing is the most dangerous one, and hearing is the least used one. In John 10:27 (KJV), Jesus said, "My sheep hear my voice, and I know them, and they follow me." I believe when we truly hear the voice of Jesus, that is when we begin to see the things around us clearly. We see how to love, how to treat one another, and most importantly, how to forgive and continue to pray for one another.

At the beginning of this project, I thought that this would be one way to make things around me better in the way that I saw it. However, the picture that I saw was something totally different now that my focus is deeper on God. I try to accept the things I cannot change in my life, but pray and ask God to change me for the things in my life. The more I hear my Lord's voice, the better I become, and the clearer I see.

I thought making known the worst of something would be better. God's love helped me realized and accept that I didn't have the perfect parents, siblings, or other family members. I didn't have the perfect pastor standing over me, speaking the Word of God that I know now would bring complete happiness in your soul. What I heard was perfect, but what I saw was imperfection. This is what brought confusion in what I was seeing because how could God's Word and imperfection go together? Then one day, he let me know that is what I work with—imperfection. You see, I understand clearly now that it's different when we error in our ways and correct the error, then, continue to walk in error and try to cover it up with God's righteousness.

Instead of allowing the things people do to frustrate me. I don't need to call them out about their wrongdoings unless I'm led by God. The voice of my Lord tells me to love and pray for them. He has their reward in his hand when he returns.

I've heard the word *love*, and he has shown me how to love. I've heard the word *forgive*, and he has shown me how to forgive. I've seen the *weakness* in man, and he has shown me how to pray. I've realized that it is not me, but the love of God that is within me.

THE CONCLUSION OF THE WHOLE MATTER

The Beginning of the End

I am nothing without him, I can do nothing without him, and I would not exist without him. I do believe that everyone was born for a purpose. Looking back over my life and the things that the Lord has brought me through, although to some, they might seem trivial and to others incredibly significant. I take them to be just as they are, my life's lessons—lessons designed by God just for me.

It is 2024, and I can say with understanding and eyes wide open that I see my path clearer each new day. I know my tour guide, "the Holy Spirit," is leading me in all truth every day to a path that will cross with others to accomplish the goal that God has designed for my life and theirs here on earth.

This book is not about me trying to point a finger to the one who is wrong or to make myself look right. We are all human, and we will continue to make mistakes until the day we leave this earth. However, I feel like what Apostle Paul wrote in Philippians 3:13–14 is true: "Brethren, I count not myself to have apprehended: but this one thing I do, forgetting those things which are behind, and reaching forth unto those things which are before, I press toward the mark for the prize of the high calling of God in Christ Jesus."

No, I do not understand everything fully, but I have learned to take each day as the Lord gives me, and his peace will surpass all understanding for the things in this world and the world to come.

What I do know is that I have grabbed hold of the hands of my Creator, and he has equipped me with someone greater than anything in this world and the wonderful thing about that it is not just for me but for anyone who wants it. I am reaching and pressing toward the mark of the heavenly prize of God, which is in my Lord and Savior Jesus Christ.

Now the conclusion of the whole matter is that my life on earth is for the purpose which I was created—not because I want to be like someone or do what someone else is doing but because I want to be who God has created me to be. He will receive all the *glory*. I believe that I will accomplish that with my salvation through my Lord Jesus Christ. This will be done by the leading of the Holy Spirit and loving everyone as he loves me.

The conclusion of the whole matter is that I am striving every day to live in the fullness of God's love and the design that he has planned for my life until he returns. My eyes are opened, and I see things differently. I see them with the understanding that love overlaps each situation. The key in everything is that I know that I am not alone. I do not have to rely only on my strength. I do not have to be concerned if I am going to be left out or if no one will recognize me for something. I no longer worry about when it will be my turn, because I know my time started the day before God placed me in my mother's womb. I do not have to worry about the hands that pressed me down or words of discouragement through my life's lessons. I know the hands that created everything are the same hands that are molding and shaping me every day, so that his prefect image will be displayed in the life that I live. I know who I am and whose I am, and I feel more than good about it.

I have more than my eyes can see and everything than my hands can touch. I want for nothing because there is nothing on earth that can place what I have in my Heavenly Father. I know he will supply all my needs according to his riches in glory. So the conclusion of the whole matter is to *live* and live life more abundantly, and the only way we can do that is to live it in our Lord and Savior Jesus Christ, by way of the Holy Ghost here on earth! And This is through the eyes of a sheep.

Each of these poems was written during a time in my life over the years. I pray they will be a blessing to you in your reading.

THROUGH THE EYES OF A SHEEP

Modern-Day Psalms

I learned to express myself with words. Words that brought comfort to my heart in a time of darkness and loneliness. These words were given to me by my Heavenly Father, who has guided me from darkness back into his marvelous light. I believed when God brought me into his marvelous light, everything would be great here on earth. I felt there would be no more pain or sorrow like I had already experienced.

I've learned that some of the hardest pain and sorrows will be found in the church. If my Lord and Savior Jesus Christ could endure the pain from those who were supposed to be in the church, so can I. When reading about the suffering of my Lord and Savior, Jesus Christ, and what he endured for mankind, which includes me, as time goes by, I've learned that as I mature and grow stronger in God, He will help me to bear the difficulties in my lifetime. No one could ever do what my Lord and Savior Jesus did for me on the cross. He bared the sins for us all and yet, in his suffering, he said on the cross, "Father, forgive them, for they know not what they do" (Luke 23:34). Some people will use you to accomplish what they want, but God will use you to accomplish His purpose, which will bring fulfillment to your life.

THROUGH THE EYES OF A SHEEP

To Be Used to and Not to Be Used For

It's so important to feel wanted.
It's so important to feel needed.
It's so important to feel love.
Especially when that love comes in the form of a dove.
It's important to understand what life has to offer.
To know what part, you have to give.
And know that you cannot begin to do until you really begin to live.
No one wants to be used or taken for granted.
To feel alone on this huge but beautiful planet.
We sometimes get caught up in this user's game.
Then when it's over, we are sometimes inflicted by its pain.
Can you remember if you were ever used?
Did you feel down and really blue?
Maybe you felt ashamed and you didn't know what to do.
Then you thought, "I'll get even. Instead of me, it will be you."
Yes, sometimes we are being used for, instead of being used to.
When it is over, we seem to be the ones who're to blame.
I am glad our heavenly Father looks down and
sees who really plays the user game.
He'll help us come above the hurt.
He'll build us up from the shame.
He'll give us strength and wisdom to know that it's really worthless...
"The User Game" Listen to His words and there you'll find yourself.
The meaning of life and what you really have to give.
He can use you to give the beauty which lives inside you.
Help you not to be used for...but to be used to...
You're not a doormat but be willing to be used
to lead someone's feet in the right path.
You're not a garbage can but be willing to be used to help someone out of their trash. You're not a blanket but be willing to be used to uncover any wrong. If you find yourself being used to helping someone in need.
To make someone feel wanted.
To make the worse person feel love.
Then you have received that Spirit that came from above.
The one that came down in a form of a dove.

It was 1981. My journey as a Christian was the beginning of a new era in my life. These were times of confusion and excitement all in one. I knew that it was the right thing to do; however, my understanding was not clear on what to do. Coming from surroundings where I felt that I had been used for other people's gain. I wanted to feel important as a person. I wanted the huff of loneliness to go away. It was a hollow space that needed filling. As a new believer, I had to trust someone, and I found myself trusting my pastor and his wife, the leaders of the church. I knew that God had placed me there because they were loving and genuine people. They not only taught the congregation about the love of God and the word of God, but they also lived the life before us. My pastor and wife were truly shepherds who watched over the sheep of God. There were times when I felt that I had to be like the crowd or my peers, but I thank God in helping me to know I only have to be who he has created me to be. To him, I am somebody.

Everybody Won't, but Somebody Will

Everybody won't praise the Most High.
Everybody won't be thankful for His Goodness
Everybody won't recognize His Mercy.
Everybody won't take out the time to stop and look around.
When in trouble instead of looking up they choose to look down.
Everybody wonders why people do the things they do.
Everybody wonders how people get things on
pretenses and knows it's not true. Everybody talks
about what's wrong rather than what's right.
And everybody doesn't think about the Creator
who made both day and night.
I am glad I am not like everybody because
somebody special would have passed me by.
I am glad I am not like everybody because He'll
take a nobody and make somebody.
So I realize that everybody will not lift Him up,
praise His name, be thankful for His goodness
or even understand His grace. No, everybody
won't but somebody will.

THROUGH THE EYES OF A SHEEP

My Stranger Secured Arms

When I was a baby, I was secured in loving arms.
Lying in a place of no danger or harm
When I was a child life seemed so easy.
Things sweet like candy were very pleasing.
When I grew older experiencing pain and hurt
I even came in contact with things that made me feel like dirt.
One day I met a Good but Amazing Stranger
He gave me hope and I was amazed to
learn he was born in a manger.
Even though life brought me sin and shame
I am glad my Stranger stopped and called my name.
He secured me with the Goodness of Heaven's love
And made me feel complete like a ball that fit into
a glove Then things began to cross my mind
Wondering if He were here with me all this time
When I was a baby, I was secured in loving arms
Instead, man's hands, the hands of my Stranger were secure
and warm. When I was a child, life seemed so easy.
Then I tasted Him it was like honey, very pleasing.
Yes, I've grown older and still experience hurt and pain
But my stranger is there to lead me through the storm and the rain.
Then the day came I learned my Stranger's name.
The one who brought me out of sin and shame
He was a God sent full of love and grace
He has assured me that as long as I am with him
I cannot be in a better place

There were times when I felt that I was too old for anyone to tell me anything. That was the time when I needed someone to wrap their arms around me and make me feel secure.

Searching

What was missing inside of me?
What made me feel incomplete?
Who was missing? What wasn't there?
To fill this emptiness of despair
I searched in my friends and we thought we knew the answers
We did friend things which involved plenty of laughter
We cried, we got mad and had so much fun
But now it's over and it's all done
Now down through the years, I realized that it was me
Not my friends, not the fun but I needed to be free.
I didn't think it was wrong to search in my friends
I just realized I needed someone who could carry me to the end
There was nothing I could find that was on this earth
Not on land, in the sea or even in the air
to move the feeling of despair.
Lying in my hospital bed on my back
I had a talk with Him, and my words were slack
But yet in all He heard was my prayer, and the
door opened, and a friend stood there.
It was like she knew what I been searching,
and she led me in the right direction
Yes, I found what was missing inside
It was His love, His peace, and His Holy Spirit that guides
I know this search must continue daily
And I know my Savior will always be there
He was missing, He wasn't there, and I am
glad He took my emptiness of despair.

When you don't meet the expectation of the world you feel that you are searching for something that will make you feel complete. What have a man who gain the whole world and lose his soul (St. Matthew 16:26)?

THROUGH THE EYES OF A SHEEP

Just to Entertain

We often see that things have changed.
People don't do what they used to They are not the same.
God has placed us in certain positions
That we may help souls in need of a new condition
So what is your goal along the way?
Is it to amuse or divert while you stand before them?
Or to reach someone who is sincere like the woman
who just needed to touch our Savior's hem.
What is your goal in winning souls?
Is it that you want them to recognize your name?
While you stand before them and entertain?
What is your goal in winning souls?
Is it to let them know that they can keep doing as they
may? Or do you inform them that Jesus *is the way!*
So if life is a stage and every soul has his part
God does not need us to perform but to reach His soul's hearts
We live in a world that time is not the same
But the God I praise never changes and He does not Entertain.

So many people want to be entertained by music, movies, plays, and even in the church. Who are we really trying to impress? "Be not forgetful to entertain strangers: for thereby some have entertained angels unawares" (Hebrews 13:2).

Who Is Your Father, Mother, Sister, and Brother?

I believe God placed us here for one another.
To help each other along the way
If we could all be still and look around,
we could see it as clear as day
You may think you have nothing to give
Maybe you feel that you're in need
But a smile or a good gesture from your heart
Will give someone just the strength to live
I believe God placed us here for one another
Because you are my father, my mother, my sister, and my brother

I truly believe that people are placed in our lives for a reason, and we learn to love them with all of our hearts. "For whosoever shall do the will of my Father which is in heaven, the same is my brother, and sister, and mother" (St. Matthew 12:50).

My Father's Car

I remember one night sitting outside on my father's car
Looking up toward Heaven watching every star
My heart was aching, and I grew very sad
Feeling lost and lonely clinging to my emotions was all I had.
Then I said a little prayer out loud
Knowing what I had said was with humbleness I wasn't proud
These words that I spoke they weren't too late
To get my life in order and start off on a clean slate
I didn't know who was listening
I just believed He was there because I felt it in my heart
There was an assurance that I wasn't just sitting outside in the dark
After I had finished my saying, sitting in
silence I could hardly hear a sound
But I had this assurance that He will always be around
Yes, I remember that night while sitting on my father's car
I am glad to know now that my Savior's ear wasn't far.

Jesus is there during the worst times of your life. The problem was I didn't know that he was there until I felt his presence covering me that night while I sat on my father's car.

Strength

Strength is when a child feels secure in a mother's arms
Strength is when a son gets a hug from his father and it is warm
Strength is when your friend gives you a helping hand
Strength is in the time of chaos and a
stranger helps you to understand
Strength is when you try and don't give up
Strength is when you can drink from life bitter cup
Strength is when you encourage someone other than yourself
Strength is when you give all when it seems nothing is left
Strength is something that is given from above
This strength is real it is God's *Divine Love.*
God will give you the desires of your heart

I thank God that I know I cannot do anything without him. "I can do all things through Christ which strengthens me" (Philippians 4:13).

4 Loves

In 1986 God blessed me with one of my deepest desire.
He united me with a good man
As I looked at him as I walked down aisle
A puzzle of my heart was added in place
It was amazing as the love we shared as we
looked upon each other's face
This man became a husband, a friend, and a lover
God placed us together, but only through him
were we able to learn from each other.
In 1987 God continued to pour into my heart
He filled a life in me with a different kind of love
As I looked upon his little face my heart overflowed with
joy God had blessed us with our first baby boy.
I never knew I could feel that type of love
But I knew that this bundle of joy was sent from God above
In 1988 a new edition was added to our lives
This was special and a wonderful surprise
As I lay in the operating room and the birth was in process
I felt uneasy and things were like a whirlwind
But when I woke up in a daze, I heard the words that
God had blessed us with a beautiful baby girl
In 1993 the last addition was placed in our lives
The same familiar feeling began to rise inside God bless us with
another bundle of joy It was another beautiful baby boy.
Now the pieces of my heart have been placed by special hands
He keeps stable and strong so I can stand
The things He does reflect from his Grace and Love
Hallelujah! Hallelujah! To my God above

When God draws you out and connects you with his Son Jesus Christ, you feel like you can conquer the world. Well, it's just not a feeling it is true. "Nay, in all these things we are more than conquerors through him that loved us" (Romans 8:37).

THROUGH THE EYES OF A SHEEP

Thank You Lord

Thank you, Lord, for a new life and saving my soul
Giving me your knowledge and the power to be bold
Thank you, Lord, for my marriage and the
increase that brought me much joy
You gave me my ideal husband, a beautiful baby
girl, and two handsome baby boys
Thank you, Lord, for the rough times
that have been a part of my life
Those were sometimes hard and felt like the blade of a knife
Thank you, Lord, for when I didn't even have a dime
Even when I felt I couldn't hold on I knew
I was yours and You were mine
Thank you, Lord, for always staying by my side
Giving me the Holy Spirit that he may be my guide
No matter what may come my way
As long as You are with me no darkness can cover my day
Thank you, Lord, for my burdens
No matter how heavy they may be
For You have assured my heart
You'll never leave or forsake me
Thank you, Lord, for all my blessing
That You have brought to me
For I know if I have patience
There is much more for me to see
Thank you, Lord, for my life and saving my soul
For out of all that you have given me
The most priceless treasure is you My heart will forever hold.

It is so good that I can talk to someone who truly listens without a shadow of a doubt. I love you, Jesus.

PAMELA RENE ANDERS COOK

A Talk with Jesus

Good Morning Jesus, how are you today?
I am glad that You are with me, to show me along the way.
I pray that You stay with me as time passes along.
For I will keep Your words hidden in my
heart that plays a heavenly song.
Good afternoon, Jesus. How Blessed it is
that your presence still lingers
Like the scent of a rose that passes like a vapor through the air
Though my eyes cannot see You, my spirit is very much aware
Again, I pray that You stay with me as time passes along
That I may have strength to stand and not walk this path alone
Good night Jesus, thank You for watching over my soul.
For keeping my family, my church, my
friends and especially my foes
Even though my enemies want me to give up, and live my life in sin,
To fail this Christian race and not endure unto the end
I know I can do all things through You Jesus, You
have given me strength time and time again
Before I close my eyes and make my words complete
Lord my soul is in your hand please always keep
For when I look upon your face
The words I long to hear you say are...
My Good and Faithful servant come home for you
have completed the true Christian race.

*Every day we live our lives according to schedules set
for our jobs, our homes, and our churches. If we don't
make it on time, things will continue as planned.*

THROUGH THE EYES OF A SHEEP

Ready or Not

This is 1998 and time is getting very late
Some people are pondering on whether it is true about the
Savior coming to place judgment on me and on you
Don't wonder, don't think, put all doubt away
Because He's coming and truly, He's on His way
This is not fiction that someone made up
Or a scene in a play where a director will say, "Cut."
Jesus is real and His judgment is true
He's on his way back to place judgment on me and on you
So ready or not He'll be here soon
You will think that this is the end
But it's really where it all begins
If you're ready you will live in paradise
If you're not you will face your doom
This world is not a stage, and this is not an act
Although this was written many years ago
Jesus is on His way and that is truly a *fact*!

Jesus said that God will send us a comforter who would bring all things to our remembrance that He has said in the word of God. "But the Comforter, which is the Holy Ghost, whom the Father will send in my name, he shall teach you all things and bring all things to your remembrance, whatsoever I have said unto you" (St. John 14:26).

PAMELA RENE ANDERS COOK

A Comfort in a Time of Need

Oh Lord, you gave me a comforter in a time of need.
When I was lonely and lost you filled my life with so much joy
No, it has not been easy, and You didn't say it would be
But in your word, you promised that you will never leave or forsake me
So I must spread the comfort that I feel inside
To help someone to know that it isn't easy
but there is a safe haven to hide
My purpose in this world is not just to live and die
It's to help someone to smile, instead of making someone cry
It's to help someone by telling the truth instead of passing out a lie
To understand the many forms of faces and pass this
comfort into their hearts of empty spaces
Oh Lord in this world it won't be easy
You did not say it would be
Please help me to remember to pass on these words of
love and strength "I will never leave or forsake thee"

I am so glad that God looks beyond our faults and sees our needs.

Praise

I praise You for your Love
I praise You for Your Kindness
I praise you for Your Mercy that took away my blindness
I praise You for Your Joy
I praise You for Your Peace
I praise You for Your Holy Spirit who abides inside of me
I praise You Father for everything that You have done
Especially giving us Your only begotten Son
Who came from Heaven to Earth, and gave Peter the Key?
That we may have life and have it more abundantly.

*Jesus is a friend indeed. "A man that has friends
must shew himself friendly: and there is a friend that
sticketh closer than a brother" (Proverbs 18:24).*

THROUGH THE EYES OF A SHEEP

A Friend while I Travel

What do I have to offer to this world?
I must see clearly to travel this road in the right direction
So when I make a mistake, I will be ready for correction
How I give is the way I will receive
How I hate is the way I will love
In order to do it right I need instruction from
someone higher who watches from above.
Some feel that the world is a bad place to be
How can that be? This world is a part of you and a part of me
So how you act when you meet a stranger, is not
always how a stranger acts when he meets you
In order to do this right, I need instructions from
someone who can teach me how to be true.
So if I meet a Friend on this way
One who cares, loves, and doesn't mind to pray
I'll consider this a blessing as I travel down this road
To find such a friend in this world is like finding pure gold.

God gives us melodies that only He can place in our hearts.

The Songs from My Children

Pain and trouble were lingering around
Nights were long and the color of the
morning sun could not be found
Seeing my children gave me strength to hold on
God used them so I could hear his sweet song
When I prayed and sought an answer from above
The enemy sent more trouble and it stayed
like a ball fitting into a glove
Seeing my children gave me strength to hold on
God used them so I could hear his sweet song
No matter how hard things may get, and the pain remains too long
Seeing my children gave me strength
God used them so I could hear his sweet song.

The song reminded me that He was there, and He would not put more on me than I can bear. No matter how things may seem, always find strength to pray. "Pray without ceasing" (1 Thessalonians 5:17).

A Hidden Love

Anger began to bury the love that I shared with my soul mate
Pride tried to step in to block the view of our fate
Resentment was not left out, for all wanted to have their part
They all wanted to steal the love that I
shared with him from my heart.
When I realized my condition, I asked for help from above
God knew what they were trying to do in our hearts
To destroy and tear it all apart
So He step in and surfaced the love that was buried and hidden
My love for him grew more every day
I still got angry, but I learned to pray
No more pride and my love for him I will not hide
Yes, we both knew in our hearts
What our God had put together designed by
His Holy words that were written
That the love we share for one another is a
love that should never be hidden.

I am glad I don't have to do anything on my own. "I can do all things through Christ which strengthens me" (Philippians 4:13).

THROUGH THE EYES OF A SHEEP

Take Control

I am blessed to see an amazing day.
Everything nice was coming my way.
I had a nice breakfast, nice words from my friends.
It felt like a beautiful flower was placed in my heart within.
Through the day things have been fine.
I should have known it would be a matter of time
I am not surprised just a little mad
He's not going to give up!
He wants everything I have.
I am blessed to see another amazing day
Everything good is coming my way
I am not worried and I am not surprised.
I am striving to reach my Heavenly prize.
Another day was given to me in a unique and special way
I realized everything good is coming my way
I am not worried, even though the world seems cold.
I am glad that I have the strength from
heaven above to take control.

*And Adam said, "This is now bone of my bone,
and flesh of my flesh" (Genesis 2:23).*

No Regrets

Remember when you said the words I love you to someone dear.
You both smiled and felt the warmth of the love that was near.
Then as time went by there was a change
When someone dear doesn't act the same
Think hard and long and remember your words
Remember who you are and remember where you are going
Then you will know that you will have no regrets

Isn't That Funny

When someone makes you happy after they've made you angry
Isn't that funny?
Funny ha ha or funny strange
When someone makes you laugh after they made you cry
Isn't that funny?
Funny ha ha or funny strange
When someone lifts you up after they have put you down
Isn't that funny?
Funny ha ha or funny strange
When someone loves just to be loved in return
Isn't that funny?
Funny ha ha or funny strange
When you find yourself in any one of these situations
Would that be funny?
Funny ha ha or funny strange.

My Life Cup

Things always seem hard, especially when
you know it's good for your life
I try not to ask why Lord, but feelings cut like a knife
Your Holy Ghost has taught me how to maintain
He has given me the strength to go on in Jesus's name
I will fight this fight and I won't give up
I am willing to help a soul so I will drink from life's bitter cup
Even though it is not always bad
For when I found You Lord, You had given me more than I had
So I will fight this fight and I won't give up
Even if it means drinking from life's bitter cup.

Success

I don't have a college degree, and I don't
look down on those who do
Sometimes they use their wisdom to share a thing or two.
I know that You are making me to be successful in Your eyes.
That I may gain wisdom from You, and not be
caught up in Satan's lies You have taught me to
encourage my children in ways to succeed
to receive from a world that is in need.
Whatever choices they choose
I pray this one thing
The first choice will be You, so You will help
them accept what this world will bring.

Your Promises

Things will not be easy
Lord You did not say it would be
Please help me to hold to my faith
Let me hope for the things I don't see.
I've asked You for my health and I've asked for wealth
But along this road I've faced whatever life has dealt.
I am not complaining, and I am not sad
I am just holding on to my hope
Believing in Your word and praying that I can cope
Things will not be easy
Lord You did not say it would be
I will hold to my faith
Believing I will receive every promise that You have for me.

Only Me

Who is to say I won't have this?
Who is to say I won't have that?
Who is to hold me back from what is good?
To discourage me when he or she could
Who is to say that you're too young?
Who is to say that you're too old?
Who is to say you cannot handle fear,
because you choose not to be bold?
Who is to say what this world has to offer?
Who is to say that you won't receive it?
Who is to say that people will laugh at your ideals?
That will cause you to stop because of what you feel
Who can hinder you? When God is for you
Who can close a door? When God has the key
Who can hinder you from succeeding?
No One can, only me.

People Say…

People say God told me to tell you this
Or God told me to tell you that.
People say you'd better do this
Or you won't be able to have that.
There are some things people say that is a statement of truth,
but it's not a true statement
You must pray to God for wisdom, knowledge, and understanding
To understand between the two
You can't live on everything that people say
Even though many try to do so
We look for different directions in ways we must go
You can't live on everything that people say
Just take time to pray and trust God to direct your way.

True Assurance

There are times when things don't always go my way
Sometimes it really feels hard especially after I pray
Disappointment comes in many forms, shapes, and sizes
But the assurance of my Heavenly Father is a greater prize.
I will not give up when my prayers are not
answered in a timely manner
Nor will I fret because the one I think will do…don't
I will hold on even tighter even when I don't
see the things, I am hoping for
I know my faith is the key to Heaven's door
So no matter how long it seems, and things still remain
the same The assurance of my Heavenly Father's promises
has been Signed, sealed, and delivered in Jesus's name.

Our Encourager

I encourage my brothers and sister that they may have hope today
I encourage those I love to hold on for help is on the way
I try to live my life, so God's light is shown
Even in the midst of the rain when the skies are not blue
No, it will not be easy, but if God can encourage me.
Then I ought to be able to encourage you.

PAMELA RENE ANDERS COOK

I Will Praise You Forever

I love you Lord.
I will praise you forever
My heart is full of your wonderful grace
I love you Lord
I will praise you forever
My mind has the knowledge from above and I long to see your face
I love you Lord
I will praise you forever
My body is empty fill me with your Holy Spirit
I love you Lord
I will praise you forever
My soul is protected by your love
I love you Lord
I will praise you forever
My heart, my mind, my body, and my soul are forever yours.

ABOUT THE AUTHOR

Pamela Rene Anders Cook was a child who did not grow up in a Christian home or on the dos and don'ts found in God's Word. Yet she believed each one of her family members had a significant part in who she is today. To be a wife, mother, and grandmother were things she dreamed about as a little girl. To her, these were the most important things. God has blessed Pamela to live in each of these roles, and she is very happy about that. She has been married to a good husband for thirty-eight years. They have wonderful sons, beautiful daughters, and lovely grandchildren.

Her walk with God has been more than she could ever think of here on earth. However, each day, the excitement that God is bringing to her has brought her to a very satisfying place of rest in him, and that is waiting for the moment when she sees him face-to-face. Until then, Pamela will live her life as the Holy Spirit leads her until that appointed time.